Minimalist Living

Off The Grid

The No Nonsense Guide to Off Grid Minimalism Living using Solar Power

Mike Holsworth

EXTRA BONUS!

Thanks for purchasing *Off Grid Living: A Beginners Guide to Surviving and Thriving In An Off Grid Lifestyle.* As a bonus and thanks, we want to provide you with additional information and content on an on-going basis.

Subscribe <u>now</u> and to learn **10 Ways to Downsize Your Current Life – and SAVE MONEY!**

Choose the NEW YOU
www.bit.ly/offgridoffer

Simply type the above link into any web browser on any device.

Don't forget,

if you like my book,

or even if you don't,

I want to hear about it!

I encouraged you to leave

A review on Amazon.

Help others decide to buy!

Solar Power

Making the Smart Switch to Solar Power – And Staying Within Budget!

Mike Holsworth

Table of Contents

Introduction

The subject of Solar Power is one that is as wide as it is deep. It covers technical, electrical, structural, and aesthetics. From the bolstering of your roof truss, to the wiring of the system and the ventilation of the batteries, the installation of the solar power system in your home may sound overwhelming and daunting, but it really is quite straightforward. There is no artistic talent required, as most of the things that go into it can be outsourced or lifted from existing plans. In this book, we introduce you to electricity and the things that you need to know about it to have a confident conversation with the people that would be setting up your system. We want to bring you up to speed on the terminology, and the benefits of the system, as well as the things to look out for when the installation starts, or the design is being contemplated.

To most people electricity is just something that powers their phone. We try to introduce electricity in a way that is not overwhelming but makes sense to you, for the purpose of getting on the path to cleaner, more independent energy generation.

We also look at the math behind the decision to

switch to solar. The best way I can save you money is not by telling you which is the cheapest system to get or the store with the best bargain, but to tell you how to come to the decision to get one or not to. It all depends on where you live and how much energy you use, and of course how much you pay.

I will guide you through a detailed economic analysis of how to determine your energy consumption profile, and how to calculate the economic sense of getting (or not getting) a solar system. It all comes down to the numbers, unless there are other qualitative considerations that one needs to make, such as constant breakdown or power outages in the area. In which case, those concerns supersede the economic decision-making process.

We will then look at the various terminologies that you will frequently come across in the area of photovoltaics. Not all of it will be referred to in the book, but this glossary of terms does two things. First, it gives you an understanding of the concepts involved in photovoltaics; and second, it gives you an overview of areas that you could possibly research beyond the scope of this book.

We then get into the meat and potatoes of the book by looking at the solar equipment that makes up the circuit in the home. The largest and most visible part of the setup is obviously the panels that you see on top of buildings. But beneath that, sometimes in the attic or other times in the basement or garage, there is a whole host of equipment that includes everything from batteries to junction boxes, and cables that complement the setup. We explain each and every item that is needed, and we talk about how you should go about choosing these items if they are not coming to you in a kit.

As you get underway, there are also some other considerations that you should make. Think about your own level of expertise when it comes to installing major equipment and then think about the fact that installing a PV system may be simple, but it is not like plugging in a light bulb. There are a lot of things to think about, and while we cover a number of them here, it is prudent to have a licensed and affiliated technician do the work.

You may also want to consider the business end of it, and there are some banks that wouldn't be opposed to giving you a personal loan or even a business loan depending on your credit standing and affiliation to the bank.

A business loan? Well, you will be surprised. There

are lending institutions that will be willing to finance the full installation of the system just so that you could sell power back to the utility company. This would be a valuable resource to look into because a loan at preferred rates could make all the difference in financing a robust system that could then sell power back to the utility company, so you will not only save on your utility bill, but you will also have the opportunity to get paid for harvesting the sun. That alone could help you to pay off the loan, and after that have extra income.

But there are a few things you have to do before that can become a reality. You will have to check with the local utility company if they are willing to buy your power, and if so you need to find out what the limitations are, if any. Some utilities have periods of time when they will not buy back power, and other times they will. There are also utilities that will not pay you for it but rather net your month's bill, or at worst case carry the credit forward. All this will dictate if you want to run energy production as an income generator and if you can get a loan to do this.

Having said that, it's time we get started on the book and get to know the preliminary information to understanding electricity, photovoltaics, and the economics of setting up solar power at home.

Chapter 1: What is Solar Power?

We hear about solar power in increasing frequency these days and that is because of two core reasons. The first is the environmental impact of non-renewable energy production and the fear of the depletion of that source of energy has expedited the development of alternative power generation technologies. This leads to the second reason, which is the precipitous fall in costs associated with the deployment of distributed solar-generated power.

The key factor that we must distinguish when it comes to understanding any kind of power generation technology is that power is not just influenced by the generation of it, but also the distribution of it. Right now, the power eco-system is characterized by centralized generation (regardless of the method of generation) that is then fed to a nationwide grid and transported over long distances. This has a two-pronged effect. The first is that it needs a huge capital investment to expand or maintain this grid. The second is that there are significant inefficiencies at play here. You have to generate a significantly higher amount of electricity to support the needs of a community when you need to transport that energy over wires, because a large amount is wasted in transmission. Look at it this way, if water pipes were naturally porous (this is hypothetical to drive a point) then you would lose more water the longer the pipe distance (traveling from source to use). So, you would lose less water if the source of water were two doors away compared to how much you would lose if the source was two towns away. Because each length of pipe the water travels, part of it seeps out of the pipe. Because of this, the water plant has to process more water to overcome the loss of this water. Processing water is expensive.

Now think about this same thing in electricity terms. The power generation company has to generate more electricity than is actually being used because it has to transmit that electricity over inefficient cables over long distances.

Since there are two factors at play here, there are two ways to reduce the burgeoning power generation cost and the environmental cost that the old way imposes on us. The first is to convert the methods of generating electricity. This is the kind of thing that Elon Musk has invested in (SolarCity – a company owned by Musk's cousins).

The idea behind this is to have a farm of solar panels and then connect that power generation ability to the existing grid so that the power can be transmitted to the end user.

The second method of doing this is to distribute the solar generation ability and allow each end user to generate what he needs, when he needs it, and then push what he doesn't use back to the grid so that others can use it. This is the personal solar generation capability.

In this book we will be focusing on this personal generation capability and how to go about literally getting off the grid by doing that.

Two Kinds of Solar Power

As the name suggests, solar power is power that comes from our sun. It is rather simple and it can be broken down into two. The first is the use of the photons that the sun releases and the second is to use the heat that the sun releases. They are not one and the same. To prove this to yourself, think about it this way. You know those tinted glass sheets that you stick on windows. Remember how it does two things. It reduces the light that comes in, but more importantly it cuts out the heat. That's because it allows the photons of a certain frequency in but filters the heat out. So, from here we know that there are at least two components to sunlight (there are more, but that is outside the scope of this book).

The first kind of energy that you get from the sun is the photon that carries light, and when you place a photovoltaic sheet in its path, the photon that hits it release the electron in the sheet. That electron then flows to wherever you want it to along the cables that are attached. In that form you get direct conversion of energy from the sun.

The second is the heat that the sun emits. This is a kind of energy too, but it is a little different from flowing electrons (which we call electricity). Solar panels that extract heat use that heat to raise the temperature of water, and that hot water is run through radiators and water tanks for showers. These are closed systems and can be used during the day, but need to be supplemented with another heat source during the night. We will get to that as the book unfolds, but for now the point that we are trying to make is that you should look at solar power as two distinct types – electron generation for electricity, and heat capture for temperature modulation.

Terminology

Cell

Cells are the fundamental components of every solar module and can be found in almost all designs, regardless of the manufacturer. It is akin to a battery cell in that it is the smallest structural unit of the battery.

CO2

See Oh Two – we all know what that is – it is the chemical abbreviation for Carbon Dioxide, which is a gas that is a product of respiration in all living tissue and it is the byproduct of combustion. In the context of energy, Carbon Dioxide will typically refer to the emissions created by the combustive processes of a system.

Conversion Efficiency

Conversion Efficiency is the term used to determine the efficacy of the equipment. It measures the amount of light photons that are converted to electricity. Both are theoretical values based on what we have observed. We can calculate how much photon is entering the system based on the exposed area and the intensity of the light (as well as the frequency of the light). We then measure how many electrons are generated by setup. The number of electrons is calculated by measuring the amps generated. The resulting ration is then expressed as a percentage of one to the other. The more efficient a system is the more electricity you can generate for the cost of the system.

Crystal

Crystals in solar terminology refer to the arrangement of atoms in a structure that is neatly aligned in the x, y, and z axes. Crystals are typically solid and have repeating patterns of short chains. They are elements used in the system of solar power generation. A crystal is a solid with molecular building blocks, such as atoms or ions, that have arranged themselves in an identically repeating pattern along all three spatial dimensions.

Energy Payback

This is an interesting term because it is rather convoluted if you don't stop to think about it. Panels require energy to construct. Manufacturers calculate the amount of energy it takes to make these panels, and then they calculate the amount of electricity the panel can generate and divide how much electricity is used to manufacture it by the amount of electricity it can generate in a year. The resulting number is the number of years it will take to breakeven in terms of the electricity used and the electricity generated.

Grid Connected

In cases where there is excess capacity generated by the solar generator, the excess energy can be sold back to the utility company via the grid. If you are off the grid, then you can't sell the electricity back to the utility company and your excess will be wasted. But if you are grid connected, then you can direct the system to push it back to the grid. For instance, this is truly beneficial when you are away on vacation and your consumption is minimal and the bulk of the electricity generated can be sent back into the grid.

Inverter

If you are grid connected, then you need an inverter to convert the DC current that the solar system generates into AC (Alternating Current).

Micro Inverter

There are also such things as Micro-Inverters and these are for smaller loads and are typically installed in individual panels to execute the conversion immediately after electron generation at the panel.

String Inverter

These are the most common of the inverter family and are typically used in residential systems to convert DC to AC.

Central Inverters

These do exactly the same thing as we have

described, but are typically used in much larger commercial photovoltaic systems.

Insolation

Insolation (not to be confused with insulation) is the measure of the amount of energy radiated by the sun in a certain geographical location. You see, one of the things that affects the density of photons to hit the surface of the earth is the angle in which it hits – that angle depends on the latitudinal position that is being measured. It also makes a difference if the light is direct or diffused. Strong insolation refers to higher density of photons, and as such it is better for photovoltaic systems. As an example, Alaska and parts of Canada have some of the lowest insolation, as opposed to say, Florida or Texas, which has higher insolation. Insolation also changes during the year, as the sun makes an apparent move into the north during summer and south during winter.

kWh

kWh stands for kilo, meaning thousand; Watt, the measure of power; and hour, the period of time it is measured in. It is the unit of energy that most current and power consumption is measured by. A kilowatt-hour is the use of 1000 Watts of energy in an hour. You know the measure of a light's wattage – let's say 100 watts. Imagine using ten of those 100 watt bulbs for an hour – that is a consumption of one kWh. When you pay your utility bill, the amount of power you consume is measured in kWh and charged at cents per kWh.

Micron

This is a measurement in the metric system. Similar to the American measurement of millionth of an inch, a micron is a millionth of a meter. In cell production, manufacturing steps occur in dimensions measured in microns.

Module

A PV module, or Photo Voltaic module, is a group of PV cells that have been electrically tied together. These modules are what are usually referred to as solar panels. Each module is covered to protect it from weather, typically with tempered glass.

MW

MW stands for megawatt, or 1000 kilowatts, or one million watts.

Net-Metering

This is more of an accounting term than it is an electrical or photovoltaic term. But it does nonetheless become relevant if you are pushing electricity back into the grid through your utility. As the term suggests, it nets out what you take versus what you send back. You could use a certain quantity of electricity during the month (let's call that X) and you could also be producing power which you send back to the grid (let's call that Y). The net would be X minus Y. Your meter will turn one way when you use the power company's electricity in one way, and it will turn in reverse when you send electricity back. You will literally turn back the meter by doing this, and what happens is that your monthly bill gets reduced by that amount. Most utility companies will carry forwards the difference, if there is an overhang, rather than send you a check for it.

Photon

You will be hearing a lot of this word. In fact the chapters preceding this have already introduced the term. Photons are particles of light. Think of it as a ball – when the light leaves the sun on its way to the earth (and everywhere else) it sends out trillions of these light 'balls'. When a photon hits a PV panel, or the cell, that photon knocks an electron off the surface and that electron then travels out of the module.

Photovoltaics (PV)

Photovoltaics refers to the generation of electricity by light. The term photo means light, and volt refers to the electricity potential.

Polycrystalline

Poly indicates many. Crystalline refers to the silicon crystals that are used in the cells of the PV panels.

Silicon

Silicon is a Periodic Table element that is the fundamental ingredient in the construction of PV cells. In essence, it is what makes sand and is the main ingredient in glass and computer chips.

Silicon carbide

Silicon carbide (SiC), is a compound that is made using Silicon and Carbon (also another member of the Periodic Table). It is an abrasive used extensively in the manufacturing of panels in the PV industry.

Stand-alone system

This is a solar system that is not feeding excess back to the grid. In fact, it is not even connected to the grid. These are what we usually refer to as off-grid systems and are self-sufficient. They store the electricity generated in batteries and used when the photovoltaic panels do not get enough sunlight to generate the required power.

Wafer

A wafer is a slice of silicon disc which forms the start of the manufacturing process of the cell.

Benefits of Solar Power

Solar power is significantly beneficial when you look at it from a scaled perspective – meaning it has overreaching benefits for all of mankind and the rest of nature because the conventional sources of electricity generation have a negative impact on the health of living organisms and on the environment as a whole. Solar energy is able to generate electricity in a way that does not have any of these effects and that makes clean energy a significant reason for the shift to it.

But more importantly, there is one economic reason that most individuals and societies fail to realize. Non-renewable resources are coming to a point where supply certainty is coming into question. Mining costs and exploration costs are increasing to the point that other forms of energy extraction are becoming comparatively less economical, and thus more expensive. That increased cost affects everyone. It translates to higher input costs for manufacturing and thereby higher costs of goods ranging from food to clothing, and transportation to housing. Indeed, it touches all layers of the economy.

Aside from rising costs, there is the annoying instability of costs that affect households. The cost of power can fluctuate as time goes by and as average temperatures start to rise, the cost of cooling homes and offices are starting to place a demand on the power grid. There are cases where you observe rolling brownouts in neighborhoods with sweltering heat in the summer. A house fitted with supplemental solar power is not going to be a victim of those brownouts, or out and out power disruption.

Often, we limit ourselves to what we want to use in the home that may place a strain on the costs of power. With a solar system in the house, we no longer have to limit our use of electricity because the electricity we demand is not derived from a non-renewable source, and so the increased demand we place has no adverse effects on the planet, our neighbors, and our future generations.

Chapter 2: What is Electricity?

As prevalent as electricity is, it is surprising to know that most people misunderstand electricity, its source, its composition, and essentially everything about it. The detailed understanding of electricity is not entirely necessary to appreciate the use of solar systems, but a cursory understanding of it will help give your understanding of solar system a better context to develop a feel for it and how solar power can be of use to you and your home.

What we want to know more about is the electricity that flows through the wires in our house and powers up our TV and Wi-Fi system, charges our phone, and turns on the light to illuminate our living space. The other kinds of electricity and derivations of it are way beyond our interest and the scope of this book. I mentioned it anyway, so that for those of you who wanted to know, there is so much about electricity, its form and its characteristics that exist beyond what you get from the wall socket.

Having said that, there are a few fundamentals of electricity that you should get to know. And that's where we will begin.

The first thing that you should remember as you proceed is that electricity is the flow of an electrical charge. That charge needs to be carried by something, and that something is typically the electron. So if you refine the definition we have so far – electricity is the flow of charge carried by an electron.

So, what is an electron? That's the easy part! Just reach back to high-school physic and you should remember that an atom is made up of three things – the proton, the neutron and the electron. Notice how electron sounds similar to electricity. The proton and the neutron of an atom reside in the nucleus and the electron rapidly orbits the nucleus in all three planes – xy, yz, and xz. Each element is defined by the number of protons it has in the nucleus – the first element, Hydrogen, has one proton, the second element, Helium, has two protons, the third element has three protons and so on. Protons carry a positive charge and are attached to neutrons in the nucleus. The neutron, as the name suggests, is neutral and does not carry a charge.

The nucleus structure is fairly simple – they are all clumped together and the more protons and neutrons there are, the larger the nucleus and the heavier the atom. Makes sense so far, right? The electrons, however, don't all share the same orbit. There is a predictable layering of these electrons. The first set of electrons orbit the closest to the nucleus and then the next orbit above that and the next above that, progressively increasing in distance from the nucleus. These are called higher energy levels, or shells. The outermost shell holds a number of electrons, and these are called the valence electrons as they form the shell that can easily accept electrons or release electrons. When they release electrons, the atom becomes a positive ion, because there is more positive charge from the fixed number of protons in the nucleus, but fewer electrons in the shells, making the balance tip in the positive direction. In the event there is space in the outer shell and an electron is brought in from elsewhere then it becomes a negatively charged ion, since there are now more negatively charged electrons than there are positively charged ions.

We talked about electricity as the movement of charges, and we said that electrons carry these charges. So, what are charges? Charges, positive or negative, which are measurable, are a feature of matter. Just like mass is a property of matter, charges are a property of matter as well. And since you can quantify how much mass exists in something, you can also quantify how much charge there is in something.

So now that you know that the electron is the one carrying the charge we need, the question then becomes, how do we get it to move down a piece of copper? Well, it turns out, when we just get into the large pool of copper atoms in the wire there are so many valence electrons available to us that we just need to knock one out of place, and when that one electron is floating around it knocks the valence electron of another atom out of place and takes its place, and that electron that was just knocked off its outer shell is floating around, it knocks into the next atom, and so it continues down the chain.

That movement of the electron is called a current. More specifically, it is called an electric current.

In order to set you up to understand how energy consumption is calculated and how the solar system works, there are three more areas of electric current that we will introduce here: Voltage, Amperes, and Ohms – those are the three terms that are used in measuring potential, current, and resistance, respectively.

Remember we said earlier that electricity is the

movement of charge. To push a charge in a specific direction, the charge has to be greater on one side than the other so that the electrons carrying the charge can go from the side that has the greater charge to the side that has the lesser charge. That's a circuit. The difference between the greater charge and the lesser charge is called the Voltage, named after Italian physicist Alessandro Volta who discovered the relationship and invented the first chemical battery.

When there is a difference in charge, and that difference is great, it corresponds to a flow of electrons in the circuit. As the charge dissipates and it starts to reduce, the difference between the two sides begin to equalize and the flow of electrons starts to reduce – just like when a battery in a flashlight starts to go flat and the light begins to dim.

When the voltage pushes these electrons through the circuit, we can measure the amount of electrons that flow through in a given period of time. Specifically, in the period of one second, the movement of 6.241×10^{18} electrons through one point in the circuit represents 1 Ampere, or amp. And that is the measure of the flow of current.

Finally we have resistance. Anything that impedes the

movement of electrons across a circuit offers resistance. Resistance is calculated in Ohms. By definition, 1 Ohm is the amount of resistance you get when you use 1 Volt of electricity to move 1 amp of current. There is a simple relationship that you should commit to memory. Remember that V stands for Volts, I stands for current and R stands for resistance. And the relationship is this $V=I*R$; $I = V/R$; and $R = V/I$.

With that, you now know enough to get you through the rest of this book.

Calculating Energy Consumption

Consumption is a factor of two things, power and time. The whole thing boils down to how much power you use for how long? Running a microwave oven for 2 seconds consumes less than running a bulb for a year.

If you want to know how much an appliance consumes, then what you have to do is find out the appliance's wattage and how long you have it on for. So let's say you take the power that the appliance consumes (which you can find in its manual or on a sticker at the back) it is the number that is given in Watts, or W. So, let's say you take a bulb that is rated for 100 Watts, and you multiply that with the number of hours that appliance is operating for. Use the hour timescale, and so if you use it for 30 minutes, you would use 0.5. If you used it for 90 minutes, you would use 1.5, and so on. The point is that you use the hourly timescale. Then you take the power in watts and multiply it by the time in hours and you are left with Watt-hours. So if that 100 Watt bulb is on your patio and you leave that on at night for 10 hours, you would then calculate your energy consumption at 100 Watts x 10 hours and that would give you 1000 Watt-hours.

The price of electricity from the pole is typically priced at cents per 1000 Watts. One thousand watts is termed as kilowatts. Kilo meaning thousand. On average in the United States 1 kilowatt-hour costs about 12 cents, but this can vary in season and area.

That bulb out on that patio used up 1000 Watt-hours and to convert Watt-hours to kilowatt-hours, just divide by 1000. And so, you would get 1 kilowatt-hour from 1000 Watt-hours. Using the average price of electricity, that means every day that you leave that bulb on it costs you 12 cents. In a month, that costs

$3.60. You can do this for every appliance and electrical item in the house and add it up to get a consumption profile. Your microwave oven that you may typically use for a few minutes at a time each day uses 800 Watts, and if you used that for a total of 12 minutes per day, then that would add up to about 60kWh per year. One of your home's highest consumption comes from your water heater, if you have it. That is rated at 4000 watts and if you just used it for 15 minutes in a day that will still add up to 365 kWh per year.

The reason you need to get to know this specific calculation is so that when you plan on a solar system in your home and RV, you would have to take in a number of factors in determining its output, so that you will be able to have output that can keep up with your daily use.

Determining Average Use

When you start the process of setting up your solar system there are three things you want to start with. The first is the average seasonal consumption that you use. The best way to do this is to check your utility bill and separate your full year into four seasons. Don't look at the total cost of the bill just yet, look for the consumption in each month and check the period of the bill. Then divide the usage into the number of days that the bill represents. So, let's say in your town, the meter man checks the meter on the 1st of every month. That means in some months you would have 30 days, others you would have 31 days as the period of the bill. Take the consumption of that period and divide it by the days of the bill. Let's say it's summer and in May, with 31 days, the consumption was 1030 kWh. That means your average daily usage was 1030/31. That works out to be 33.22 kWh per day.

Do this same thing for every month of the year, and if you have records for the last few years, you should put them together on a spreadsheet. Once you do this, set the months of the years across the top line of the spreadsheet and fill in the corresponding months of consumption. So below the January header, for instance, place the average daily kWh usage for Year 1, then below that place the number for Year 2, and below that, for Year 3. Ideally, they should be the numbers of the immediately preceding three years. Three years should suffice because anything older than that and it may skew the numbers too much.

Once you have that, in the next line calculate the average of the three numbers. So, let's say your average daily usage for January 2015 was 23.22; the average daily usage for January 2016 was 23.86; and your average daily usage for January 2017 was 24.18. In the line below those three numbers add the three averages and divide that by the number of years - in this case that would be 3. It would look like this - 23.22+23.86+24.18 = 23.75kWh per day. Do this for every month of the year and you will find your household's average daily use of electricity by month.

Now look at the maximum and look at the minimum of those numbers across the year and you will get the idea of your range of usage. This average use profile will vary for each of you because it is a function of habits, climate, demographics, family size, and so on.

Understanding your range will give you an idea of the output that you will need to install in your home, and if you will be able to sell the excess electricity output during the months that your consumption is low.

Chapter 3: Mobile Power Set Ups

Thus far we have been looking at power generation for the home. That is a fixed asset consumption. That's your base and it is something that you will also use for charging all your mobile equipment. Just think about your phone, for instance – it is a mobile unit that you use your home base to charge.

In the same way you need to keep all your other equipment charged or you need to have mobile power units – like mobile solar units or generators to keep them operational when they are away from a plug-in source of power.

Battery Packs (rechargeable)

Battery packs are just a bunch of batteries packed together and are used as convenient portable power sources. Instead of having one battery that may be just 1.5 volts, you could put ten of them in series and have a battery pack that is 15 volts, or you could put them in parallel and have them still output 1.5 volts but last for a longer period of time.

In most cases, battery packs that you buy at the store to keep your phone charges when you are on the go are a bank of batteries tied together in parallel so that they constantly provide the charge you need but do so for a longer period of time. They are usually rated in terms of mAh which is mili-Amp hours.

In the same way that you have this little battery pack that can be recharged for your small electronic devices, you also have battery packs that you can use to power up larger equipment. Depending on the equipment, you would typically either need to charge them at home or have solar charging stations that you can use. The best way to choose these battery packs would be to determine the output needed, how long it will take to charge the item or power the item, and the cost.

When you set about buying one of these battery packs you need to find out how many cycles they will be good for. A cycle is the charge and discharge of the battery. When you charge it to full power and then use up that power by discharging it, that is one cycle. Manufacturers typically test these batteries extensively and know with good approximation how many times you can charge and discharge these batteries. They will tell you the projected number of cycles that you can reliably use the packs in the manual or the specifications.

Do also look out for other information when it comes to rechargeable packs. The main issue is safety, and these packs can have explosive characteristics if they are not properly used according to the manufacturer's instructions. For this reason, never buy a pack that has no paperwork or has instructions that are in a language that you do not understand. Never charge them until they overheat, and in many cases, manufacturers will advise you to discharge the battery fully before recharging them. Adhere to this closely. You may want to purchase a discharging device to fully discharge the battery so that you can charge it whenever it is convenient. There are designs (more expensive ones) where there is a circuit in the pack that will discharge the battery whenever you plug it in before it starts to charge the battery.

Mobile Average Usage

In the same way that you profiled your home's average usage, you need to do the same with all your mobile equipment. This is not limited to your phone. It includes your vehicle – your car, boat, RV, and so on. You need to get a calculated profile for what your energy consumption is for all these so that you can develop a comprehensive profile of your power consumption needs. This does two things. This will determine if your solar system in the home is set up to handle these loads, and if they aren't you could increase the requirement – even if you are planning to get a boat or an RV sometime in the future.

The second is that it determines the basis of your energy setup. That means you could possibly choose to have separate systems for the RV or the boat. RVs have surface area on the roof to have their own solar panels, instead of having large banks of batteries beneath the vehicle for extended use between RV stops.

To do this, make a list of all the vehicles you have that require electric power and check with the manufacturer on the profile of use for that specific model and vehicle under the condition that you typically use them in.

Once you have these profiles handy, you now have a

usage profile that is comprehensive. From your home to your portable devices, to your vehicles and other mobile equipment. This ensures that you have the right goal for power generation when it comes to setting up your solar system.

Chapter 4: Solar Equipment

The second half of this book now deals with the choosing and setup of your solar equipment. You have an objective to reach and that objective is defined by the average and peak usage of your profile determined in the first half of the book.

Before getting anywhere near the design, ask yourself if there are going to be batteries involved. If there are batteries involved, your design considerations will change. If there are no batteries involved, there will be something else, and it automatically means that you will have a hybrid system that draws power from the main utility whenever there is insufficient power in the system.

Because solar panels are modular, they are scalable and you can typically add on more panels when the need arises or when economics allows, you can ramp up your purchase over time. But there are ancillary considerations that you need to keep in mind when you do this. You should get the infrastructure set for the full requirement that is needed. Take for instance if you need to fortify your roof structure for the installation of the panels. Don't just fortify it for the initial number of panels – fortify the structure for the number of panels that you need to have for your peak usage. The same goes for the wiring and the other infrastructural items.

When you start the design phase, know your full peak requirement and then iterate the need until you come to a balance of what you need (plus a little extra) and how much you can afford.

You need to figure two aspects of the economics of solar installations. You have the cost for the panels which are modular, and you have the cost for the infrastructure, which is a little more cumbersome; and you may want to set up the infrastructure to handle more so that you don't have to tear things down to increase capacity.

Selecting Solar Panels

Solar panel selection is just as much an economic exercise as it is a technical one. You need to be able to look at both in your planning stage and find the optimal balance of the two considerations. The best system for you is not likely the best system for your neighbor.

The first step in selecting a solar panel is to understand your usage profile – and you have already done that.

The next thing is to determine the kinds of solar panels you will need, and in this regard there are three things you will be looking for. The first is that you need to understand the solar panel's efficiency. Do not think that the most efficient solar panel is the most effective. The efficiency of the panel as determined by the manufacturer is just the efficiency of the conversion of sunlight to electricity. This makes a difference depending on where you live. The less sunlight you get, the more efficient you want it to be so that you can pull every last amp out of the system. But highly efficient systems also get expensive really quickly and that is the final determinant of if that makes it effective for your situation. The industry average for efficiency that you should look for when choosing solar panels is between 16% and 18%, and then normalize that with the costs involved over a 10 year period.

The next is to look at the warranty provided by the manufacturer. The industry average in this regard is between 10 and 25 years. Once again, temper the longer horizons with a cost factor.

To make things simple, make sure that the manufacturer provides you with the quality that adheres to the IEC61215 standards rather than just a random guess at how durable or how efficient it is going to be. The IEC is the International Electrotechnical Commission, which has performed rigorous stress tests on solar panels and developed the reliable standards homeowners can turn to.

There are three categories of panels you can categorize that are available in the market today. Simply, they are economy, standard, and premium. Think of it this way – BMW, Honda, and a Geo Storm. The BMW gets you from A to B, and has all the bells and whistles but costs a pretty penny. The Geo Storm on the other hand gets you to all the places the BMW can, costs a fraction of the price but... well, you get the idea. When you don't have the resources to get the BMW, go ahead and work with the GEO. It gets the job done.

The third aspect that goes into solar panel selection is the economics of it. This is when you do a spreadsheet to crunch the numbers. Here is how you do that. Start with the Warranty period and if you have a ten-year warranty then use that as a guide.

Think about a ten-year horizon for the use of your panel. Use your Average use numbers from the last chapter and increase them by 1% each year (this is a modest increase). If you have a 22-kWh average daily usage in January of 2018, then take that and add 1% to it. You can just multiply 22 *1.01 and that will give you 22.22 for January of 2019, and 22.44 for January of 2020. You do that for each month. If February 2018 is 21.9, then February of 2019 will be 21.9*1.01, the following February will be 22.12 and the following February will be 22.34. Project this out for 10 years.

At the bottom of each month's daily average, multiply the number of days in that month. So January of 2019 would be 22.22*31, which will be 688.82 kWh for the month of January 2018. In the line below that, multiply it by the cost per kWh in your area. For this example, I will use the rate of $0.12. As such my cost of electricity for January 2018 in this example is $82.65. Do that for all the months in the ten-year period.

What you have now is a cost profile of your energy use for the next ten years. This is the number that you want to improve on. If you do not spend a penny on any changes or add any equipment, this is a pretty accurate depiction of the energy you will use. With that you now have a good idea of how much you want to spend on the system that is to be installed. If you added up all the monthly uses for the next 120 months, that should give you approximately $11,000 (this is not an accurate number). But this number tells you one thing. It says that if you were to completely rip out your dependence on the grid and put in a totally independent system that can handle the peaks of usage and stay stable for ten years, the most expensive system you could pay for would be $11,000. That's the theoretical limit you should want to spend. Of course, you need to discount that number because you will be paying that upfront instead of spreading out monthly over the next ten years. If you discount it by 2.5% annually to adjust for the purchasing power of today's dollar, then what you should spend $11000 for over the next ten years, you should only spend $8600 for today. That should be the cost of your system. Here is how you get that number - $11,000 / (1.025^{10})$. If your situation is different, and I am certain it will be, replace the 11,000 with the number you get after adding up all the monthly electricity costs you will be paying over the next ten years. If you wish to calculate 15 years, then add up 15 years' worth of utility bills and change the exponent in the denominator to 15. That gives you the budget you should spend on for your unit.

There are a few things that you need to watch out for here. The first is that this total price should include everything that you need to do to get the system to turn on and supply you with uninterrupted power. If it is purely a system without batteries for night use, then you need to reduce the amount by how much you think you will spend on power usage at night.

This simple exercise should give you an idea of how to think about the economics of conversion. If you extend that to 25 years, then the total number increases by that much. This gives you the total amount you should spend on everything, not just panels. Make sure you get all the costs included before you start making purchases.

Most people do not do a total tear down and replace their entire dependence in one go. It is not unheard of, just not common. Ideally you would find a way to replace about 40% of your consumption and that would be during the day. You would still feed off the grid for night usage, as batteries can get expensive very quickly and you need to factor that in. There are a few companies that are developing storage systems so that you can store the power generated during daylight hours and then use that at night –but the economics is not quite there yet. You can still do it, but that would be for environmental considerations only and not so much for economic reasons, since they would actually cost more to do that.

Selecting Solar Charge Controllers

The first thing you need to know about a solar charge controller is that it is the key piece of equipment in the whole setup. It is what keeps the batteries optimally charged and extends their life while giving you the reliability you need. There are two kinds of controllers that you will be faced with, from which you can choose. The first is the MPPT and the second is the PWM.

MPPT stands for Maximum Power Point Tracking and it is the one that is more efficient and versatile. You know the effect of connecting a power source in series or parallel from back in Chapter 2. Well, the MPPT allows you to connect the panels in the solar array in series, thereby allowing higher voltage out of the system. Following Ohm's law, the higher the voltage, the lower the wattage, and that means that the infrastructure to support the installation can use longer but smaller gauge cables. The system becomes more efficient overall and the batteries can be tied in easily.

When choosing a controller, the first thing you would think about is the number of solar panels there will be in the array and the wattage that they produce. The second thing that you would need to consider are the batteries that you would have in the system, be it 12, 24, or 48 Volts (the exact voltage you use would then depend on the inverters).

Now, for a little bit of math. According to Ohm's Law, Current multiplied by Voltage results in wattage. In other words Watts = Volts x Amps. With this equation, if you raise the wattage, and the volts are stagnant, then you would reduce the amps to compensate, as mentioned earlier.

So, if you know the amount of wattage in your solar panels – let's say that's 3000 Watts, and you have a 48-volt battery, then your amps would be 3000/48 which would be 62.5 amps. Now you know what rating controller you would need. You should typically get something that is a little higher than the calculated number, so in this case you can choose between what is typically out there, which is 60, 80 or 100 amps. Since you need 62.5, you would choose 80 amps.

This knowledge gets you to make the rough calculations you need, but once you have done that, make sure you talk to the manufacturer of the controllers you have shortlisted and get them to suggest the controller they think will best suit your home's requirements.

The controller should be the second thing that you consider, but remember all the components you choose will be put through an iterative process based on how the design evolves and the best combination of components and cost.

Selecting batteries

There are three kinds of battery that you can choose from. Of course, by that, I don't mean you can choose them based on purely economics or features. There are certain mission-specific factors that you need to consider when you choose a battery. We will look at all three and the applications that each have.

Types

The first type of battery is the Flooded Lead Acid battery. This battery has some benefits and is popular with starter systems because they are relatively low priced. A person who is looking to leave it relatively hands-off should not be using this kind of battery, as there are a number of maintenance and ongoing care steps that you would have to conduct throughout the life of the battery. One of the most time-consuming efforts is the electrolyte replenishing that needs to happen constantly, especially if it is a high-cyclic use. It is also typically used in off-grid applications, and as such are chosen for volume rather than features. This kind of battery is also hazardous and needs to be well ventilated. Even though they are typically inexpensive initially, their maintenance costs are on the high side.

The second is the VRLA Lead Acid Battery. If you are running a hybrid system where you are on the grid and using solar power, then this battery seems to lend itself to that, unlike the first type above. It can also be used for off-grid setups, and this makes it versatile even if it does cost a little more. The flexibility it gives you when it comes to on- or off-grid does not always figure into it either one way or the other unless they are planning to ramp up their capacity over a stretch of time from a point where they still have grid dependence until they are totally self-sufficient. In that case scaling the batteries is also an option, and therefore this kind of battery will make sense. Even though they are slightly more expensive than the first type, the long-term benefits pay for themselves because the batteries are self-contained and are virtually maintenance-free, and this also means there is no need to top-up the electrolytes. They still need to have some form of ventilation, and that is not so much for the batteries but for the quality of air for those who are close by. A simple exhaust fan installation would typically suffice.

Finally, you have the Lithium-Ion battery, which are the most expensive of the three to start off with but are relatively inexpensive over the long run. In return for this high initial cost you get superior cycling characteristics that are significantly higher than the first two. It is also maintenance-free. But the issue that needs close consideration is that the batteries need to be actively managed by a separate controller to make sure that there are ideal charge-discharge cycles and that they are not overcharged or over depleted.

There are important things that you have to consider

here. The first is that you must first figure if you want to be on the grid, off the grid, and if you are going to be available at home throughout the year or if someone will be available to take care of the system in your absence.

The first two systems described above can't really be left alone, and if you plan on going away for vacation and have electricity be generated and sold back into the grid, the first two batteries are certainly not appropriate.

So, as I mentioned earlier, your battery choice depends on whether you want to be on- or off-grid. The second consideration is if you feel like you have the ability and time to mess around with the batteries or if you would like them to be self-sufficient, in which case you can stick with the Lithium ion batteries.

The one good thing that you should consider is that Li Ion batteries are starting to come down in price, and they are certainly worth the extra cost now more than ever, especially if you want a hassle-free, scalable system.

Selecting an Inverter

An inverter is an important part of the grid system or the grid hybrid system. You know those times when you switch from solar to grid power, you would sometimes get those flickers of light as there is a gap in the transition. Inverters prevent that from happening. So, unless you only use power when the sun is up and the rest of the time your house is electricity free, you are going to need to use an inverter whether you are on, off or partially on and off the grid. Unlike battery considerations, which you can choose if you want to have a battery in the system, you can't really make that determination here. You are going to need it and you need to get one that is robust. In today's world, where many of the appliances and gadgets are sensitive to power fluctuations, you want to keep your supply as stable as possible. This is where the inverter comes into play. It also comes into play when your batteries are full, there is excess generation and you want to divert the extra energy back to the grid. If you plan on doing this, then getting a quality inverter is something that becomes a must.

Here is how you go about choosing one.

There are a few types of inverters in the market and they are, again, mission specific. The first thing that you will want in an inverter is that it is programmable. If it is programmable, then you will be able to set the parameters and fly hands-free. There are also non-programmable inverters, but these are limited in their scope and are typically used when you have an off-grid system and are actively controlling what you use. Typically, you could use a system without inverters when they are standalones out in your cabin where you just need to turn on in the daytime. Even then a non-programmable inverter is not something that you want to get into, especially since the price difference is not a big deal.

Selecting Wire

Solar panel wires are typically referred to as PV wires in the industry. You need them to run from the panels in the array to the rest of your PV system, but not to the rest of the house that connects to the outlets or run your lights. The gauge of wire you use is important in keeping your design working within the parameters that you designed them for. There is a reason for this. A lot of efficiency can be extracted or lost in the path between source and use, and the wiring is the conduit for that. It can either serve to minimize efficiency on a best case scenario if done wrong, or actually be the source of catastrophic failure and damage at worst case. For this you really should rely on a licensed installer, but just so you can keep your wits about you In understanding the nitty-gritty we are going to delve into the basics of wire selection.

There are two general types of wire. The first is the classification of the number of strands in the core. That just refers to how many strands of conductor are contained within the wire. There is a single kind and there is a multiple kind. The two kinds of wire are not beneficial in one way or the other for electrical reasons so much as mechanical reasons. The single strand is better when the use of the cable will not be under constant movement or vibration. The single strand core on the other hand is used when the wire is installed in an area of high frequency movement, vibration or bending stress.

For PV installation, using either is fine because most of the wring is going to be fairly stable and so the actual consideration under this condition will be similar.

PV wires are rated by amps. Remember, amps are the measure of current flow per unit of time in one spot on the circuit. So, if you were to slice a cable, look at its cross-section and count the number of electrons (carrying the charge) flowing through that cross-section in one section that would correspond to one coulomb of charge in one second. We talked about this earlier. So it makes sense why wires are rated this way. If you want a wire to carry more charge then you would use one that does so. The higher the amps in the system, the thicker the wire's gauge needs to be. So, if you have a 7-amp system, you would need at least a 7-amp wire, but typically about 15% more so a 9-amp cable would do the job. The reason you go a little higher is so that you don't have a heating problem when running consistently at near-maximum loads.

Even if you do not plan on running at peak loads and you decide to skimp on the wiring, imagine if your wire can only carry less than what the panels are putting out, then your batteries are not going to get charged at an optimal rate, which would damage the batteries in the long run, especially when you are using Li Ions.

All things being considered you would buy the thickest wire possible, but wire can be expensive and the thicker the wire gets, the more expensive it gets, so you need to keep your overall costs low, and to do that don't spend it on the thickest wire possible.

However, if you recall earlier in the book, it was mentioned that you should plan ahead. If you plan on ramping up your system over time then you should get the wiring necessary for the system that you will end up having. So, for instance, if you are eventually planning to have a 10-amp system, but for now you are only putting in a 5-amp system, then the other equipment may be phased in over the years, but your wiring, which is the infrastructure, should be installed at 10 amps, because getting a contractor to come in, strip the old wires and put in new ones is going to be more expensive.

The next thing about wires is the length. The longer the wire is from the PV array to the batteries or from the batteries to the box, the more you need to think about increasing the thickness. When you have long wires, it is going to raise the resistance of the wire and this decreases the amps and drops the voltage. That means the batteries are going to get less juice, the appliances are going to get less power, and you are creating a fire hazard as the cables could heat up. To prevent this from happening, increase the wire rating by 35% for long installations so if you have a 10-amp requirement make it 14 amps (13.5 rounded up).

One more thing about wiring, if it is not yet obvious - when you calculate the wire gauge, you have to do it in segments. For instance, the load from the panel to the batteries is going to be extremely different than the load that runs from the box to the ceiling light. The line to the appliance may only be 7 amps but the line to the batteries from the PVB array could be 40 amps. This is something that you can save on by optimizing the wires. You can also optimize the wires by decreasing the distance between the points that need thicker wires and lengthening the distance that use thinner wires.

Having said that, you should know that there is so much about the electricity and wiring alone in the setup of a PV system, and you really should get a licensed installer and technician to do this for you. Not doing so could void the insurance on your house in the event of an electric fire.

Chapter 5: Maintaining Your Solar System

This is a fairly short chapter because it is the opinion of most professionals and most authors in this business that all major maintenance be handled by a professional. One that, preferably, was involved with the installation, but otherwise one that is qualified and licensed.

For some reason it has entered the public's cumulative consciousness that solar power installation can be easily undertaken by most people. This is certainly not true, and more importantly, this is dangerous. But as far as maintenance is concerned, there are a few things that one can do, but the rest of it should really be undertaken by a professional, as well.

Typically you should check with the installer if they have a service contract that you can sign up for. It typically involves a monthly fee that may be waived for the initial months if they performed the installation. It also makes it extremely unlikely that in the event of a warranty claim there will be any fuss, since they are the ones doing the maintenance.

So the first best bet that you can make is signing on with your installer for a service contract. When you are choosing your installer, this is one of the things you should check on and negotiate.

If you really want to get in and get your hands dirty, you can either get a kit with detailed instructions, and as long as you are handy with the necessary tools then you should be fine. Just make sure you get a licensed electrician to at least do the wiring and give it a once over before you turn things on – especially if you are connecting it to the grid.

You should still get a professional to maintain it, but there are things that you can do to keep it in tip-top condition above and beyond what the service guy does. Make sure that the panels are always clean and the glass is in good condition. Wipe them clean and if possible when you have them installed on your roof, install necessary walking up paths between the panels so as to give yourself room to clean the glass and perform upkeep maintenance.

Make sure there are no rodents in the areas where wiring runs and, if possible, run the wired in conduits and keep them out of exposure to the element and pests. Run the self- diagnostic tools if you have an automated system. Test all circuit breakers as well.

Check the manual for your particular system and keep a checklist based on the items that they recommend as the user maintenance.

Conclusion

That brings us to the conclusion of this introductory book into Solar Power. There are benefits to switching over to the use of solar power, and there are also benefits to switching over to utilities that use solar power – if you don't live near one, not to worry, that will be coming soon. But having solar power installed in your home is not just about clean energy, it is about distributed energy and weaning off the reliance from a service provider.

In addition to all the talk about solar installations, it would be wise for you to also have the system on a back-up generator so that in the event of down time, the generator can be brought online to run at least the basics in the house. It is possible to have the generator spliced into the circuit and run on a program if the operator can be controlled electronically. That way, if you are not at home, it is possible that the generator can kick in automatically.

As a precaution you should also have the technician install a failsafe, where the activation of the switch shuts everything down and moves to draw power from the grid. This can be helpful in a situation where there is an emergent problem and you don't have time to think about it. Just shut it down, turn off the system, and have the time revert to grid power.

Make sure that all power points and junction boxes are properly fused so that individual systems can be cut off the circuit in the event of a problem and that the problem does not backtrack its way to the battery bank or the other sensitive equipment. This rarely happens, especially if you have a licensed technician do the job and the wiring and equipment are properly rated.

Solar power is at its nascent stages of development, and in time not only will it be the leading method of distributed energy generation, but it will also be the leading source of energy distributed via a national grid. The current US grid is one that is old and falling apart and it needs to be fixed. It is not always felt, but when the demands for power become prevalent during the hot summers, then the rolling brownouts in many of the neighborhoods across America remind us that distributed generation is one of the richest answers to a failing national grid.

Solar power at home is not just about saving the environment. Of course, there is that. But there are some of you who don't buy into the global warming warning. But putting that aside, you have to at least think about the distributed power perspective of solar power. It is the only easily installable, easily operable, and safest technology out there that allows you to take charge of your own home and the power that feeds it.

Solar power installation is an iterative process at the planning stage and you should not feel like the repeated back and forth is a waste of time. As my grandpa used to say: measure twice, cut once, measure once, cut twice. You should apply the same philosophy to the installation of the solar system.

You should also look into the tax credits that you may qualify for or for the buy-back programs that some utilities offer. In which case you definitely want to investigate a programmable system that can feed power back to the grid during their peak consumption times.

If you are building a new home and are thinking of putting this in while the home is being built then you are on the right track. If you are designing your house from scratch, then it's a good time to beef up the support structures and have customized fittings to make the installation more aesthetic and more efficient.

One strategy you could use is to also consider short-term systems that would last you five years and are significantly cheaper. If you could install this. then the three-year payback period will still give you a breakeven and it will get you accustomed to this kind of PV driven power. In that five years, the technology of PV systems is set to skyrocket and the price is set to plummet, and you may just be able to put in a better system at a cheaper price at that point.

Off Grid Living

How To Start Your Off Grid Journey

Mike Holsworth

Table Of Contents

Introduction

Numbers don't lie. According to data released by the Organization for Economic Co-Operation and Development, poor health and a variety of diseases that stem from polluted air, water, and environmental sources are expected to steadily increase up to the year 2050.

By then, it's projected that air pollution will be the top cause of environmentally-caused deaths worldwide, that 240 million people *still* won't have access to clean, sustainable water sources, and that there will be a significant rise in deaths associated with the exposure to hazardous chemicals.

Aside from that, it's also believed that conditions like malaria, fatal diarrhea, and heat stroke are anticipated to increase because of the effects of environmental pollution on the global climate.

It truly seems like we are headed down a dark path. But who's to blame?

Should we point our finger to those billion-dollar corporations that churn out mass-produced single-use plastic by the millions every day? Should we cry foul to large commercial establishments like malls that produce sewage waste and plastic garbage at an unprecedented rate? Should we monitor and police suburban communities and households, curtailing the way they use cleaning items, personal care products, and food? Or should we look into our own personal practices and how we are wasteful as consumers?

It's easy to single somebody out and claim that *you're not the problem*, but the bitter pill we all need to swallow is that one way or another, we've all contributed to the environmental crisis.

Sure, when you think about things on an individual scale, the way you consume everyday products might not seem like a major factor. However, once you consider how almost all individuals and households feed into this dismal consumerist behavior, it's easy to understand how your own actions contribute to the global problem.

Consider asking yourself these questions - do you know where your garbage goes when the garbage collectors pick it up outside your house? When you flick on a switch at home, do you know what goes into generating that seemingly small amount of electricity? Do you know where your waste goes when you flush your toilet? Where does tap water come from and where does it end up when it all falls down into the drain?

The grid - that's what connects and collects our waste. Throughout the years, lawmakers and city planners have tried to perfect the grid. However, contrary to popular belief, the grid is far from perfect. If anything, the only thing that politicians and organizers have been able to do is to convince everyone that once you churn your waste into communal public utilities, then it's as good as dealt with.

Out of sight, out of mind.

Unfortunately, there are harsh realities behind each discarded garbage bag, every drop of wasted water, every light switch left turned on, and every single flush. But for now, what you need to know is that large-scale waste management isn't as polished as officials make it seem.

Tons of garbage and wastewater find their way into the environment, causing significant damage to natural habitats and a variety of animal species. Over the years, this accumulation of filth in natural ecosystems has caused major climate issues, which is manifested today by an increase in global temperatures.

As we continue on this downward spiral, and destroying the environment, we face the possibility of leaving an uninhabitable world for our children and grandchildren. Yes, it might seem like a farfetched reality - but it's a reality we need to acknowledge and accept.

So now, the real question is - what can *you* do to help address this dire situation? How can you reduce your carbon footprint to make an impact on the global environment? What steps can you take to make sure you contribute as little as possible or not at all to the poor waste management process that's been in operation for centuries?

Living off the grid.

To eliminate your negative impact on the world, you need to remove yourself from the grid altogether, and this means avoiding the use of public utilities like electricity, water, and sewage.

Successfully and efficiently managing your own sewage, finding sustainable water sources, and powering your home with resources you harness independently from the rest of the community means that you can control how clean it is.

Living off the grid also means reducing your carbon footprint because you *don't* depend on unreliable entities to manage your waste for you. In effect, you get to decide how to process the by-products of your household and ensure that they won't damage the environment.

Will it be easy? Absolutely not. Most of us have grown up used to a lifestyle that heavily relies on the utilities provided to us with no questions asked, so transitioning to a state of household management that relies entirely on your own capacity to manage waste can be a Herculean challenge.

Will it be worth it? Absolutely. Although there's no way to calculate just how significant of an impact your household could have on a global scale, living off the grid can be extremely beneficial because it reduces the cost of household utilities and makes you *more involved* and *accountable* for your own waste production and management.

On top of that, you would be joining a group of thousands of other households that have decided to live without depending on public utilities. And if there's anything we've learned from the current state of waste management, it's that there *definitely* is strength in numbers. Therefore, even the addition of a single household by a group of eco-conscious individuals living off the grid can make a significant impact.

It's definitely not a glamorous lifestyle, but the idea of being able to preserve the environment in your own little way can be more than enough to fuel that desire to live without needing to rely on public utilities.

So, if you've decided that you're ready to transition to a more conscious, responsible, and accountable life, then let's get started on the steps you need to take to live off the grid.

Chapter 1 - What is Off Grid Living?

Even though the concept of 'living off the grid' might seem like a revolutionary idea to many of us, it has been in practice ever since the dawn of man. Of course, modern civilization has made it much less practical to live without public utilities as they are considered far more convenient. However, there are countless communities around the globe that manage to survive and thrive without the need for waterworks, sewage systems, and electricity.

Consider native tribes and indigenous groups that still collect water from natural sources like streams and rain, that live without the need for electricity, and that survive without having to funnel their waste into a systematized water sanitation and sewage system. When you think of how they manage to do it, it's easy to see that it is *very* possible to live without having to rely on public utilities.

How Hard Will It Be?

Do you have to go *indigenous* to make it work? If you consider your impact on the environment, there are surely benefits to living off the grid, but as children accustomed to an urban lifestyle, we've all learned to love our TV shows, movies, and smartphones. So, is it possible to live with these simple joys without having to rely on the grid?

The answer is *yes* - it's very possible. While indigenous groups might be able to give us an idea of how to make the off-grid lifestyle work, we don't need to pattern our entire lives off of their methods. Remember, they don't rely on electricity because most of them never learned the value of electronic devices since they aren't typically available to them. But with the dawn of alternate energy sources like solar power, it's possible for off-gridders to still use and enjoy their devices without relying on public utilities.

Are you feeling apprehensive? Moving to an off-grid lifestyle comes with its own difficulties. And we're not going to lie - there will be a few challenges that might make your transition difficult. So, to help you better prepare for what lies ahead, consider these common challenges to transitioning to an off-grid lifestyle.

Daily Tasks Become More Difficult

Living on the grid meant you could get up in the morning, turn on the tap, and wash your face with nothing more than the twist of a knob. But living off the grid means you might have to complicate that simple three-step ritual, as well as many others.

Unless you're planning to live in total isolation, you need to understand that it's still important for you to maintain personal hygiene, especially if you're expecting to socialize. However, as you would be in charge of collecting and storing water, you might not be able to use it as freely as you're used to.

If you get water from rainfall during the wet season and your area is known to go through some nasty summer droughts, you have to be able to store enough water if you don't have alternate sources like freshwater streams.

What about food? If you experience a harsh winter in your area, you need to constantly store food for when the cold season rolls in. But if you've killed a large animal 5 months before the snow crept in, where do you store it? If you don't have a fridge, how do you make sure all of that meat stays fresh all the way to winter time?

Some Things Can't Be Done Alone

This all depends on how 'off' the grid you plan to live. There are people who simply choose to do without public utilities. However, there are others who go the extra mile and choose to be completely self-sufficient.

While off the grid and self-sufficient homes have similarities, they aren't exactly the same. Off-grid homes are simply homes that don't use public utilities, while self-sufficient homes are those that rely on themselves even for necessities like food and personal care products. So, while all self-sufficient homes are off-grid homes, not all off-grid homes are self-sufficient.

There are unique challenges to living a self-sufficient life, and many of the chores associated with it can't be done alone. For instance, for large households especially, harvesting and storing food can be time-consuming and physically demanding and require at least 2 or 3 people to get it done in time before any crops wither and die.

With off-grid homes, the biggest challenge may be collecting water. Rainwater can be caught passively as long as you have the right instrumentation set up to do it. However, collecting water from other sources might require more hands, especially if you don't have a well.

There's Going to Be Red Tape, and Lots of It

Many people claim that living off the grid is actually illegal. But is it really? First of all, solar energy isn't illegal. Building your own home isn't illegal. Growing vegetables, crops, and rearing livestock isn't illegal. On their own, these factors that contribute to off-grid living *are not* illegal and are perfectly permissible in most, if not all counties.

The issue of living off the grid arises when you consider the restrictions, city ordinances, and regulations that make living off the grid a challenge.

For instance, most of the people who want to live off the grid prefer smaller cabin homes. However, most counties will not permit individuals to build homes that are less than 500 square feet, even if it's on their own land. On top of that, residents in some places are not allowed to camp out *on their own land* for longer than 2 weeks. So, if you are planning to pitch up a tent and live in your backyard while you build your cabin home, you need a long-term camping permit.

So, just move out to a rural area, right? While that might seem like a good idea, minimum lot size restrictions grow exponentially as you move out to remote locations. In the city, you might find that the minimum lot size is around 5,000 square feet.

But as you move out towards the rural areas, counties will require that you purchase lots of at least 5-10 acres in size. If you want to cut the lot down, then you need to have what's called a subdivision, and each lot needs to be connected to a roadway and given a specific address.

Perhaps the most difficult of all restrictions to deal with is the fact that most counties *will not allow households to live off the grid.* Sewage systems, waterworks, and electricity need to be connected to your house one way or another, and most cities will not allow you to use alternative solutions. Also, if you're planning on using solar energy, your county will likely require you to be hooked up to the grid anyway.

Any surplus energy you don't use will be sold at wholesale price, and you'll get paid for what you supply to the city. While that can be enough to offset some of your expenses, being hooked to the grid also means that you might end up using traditional electricity if you don't end up producing enough solar power, defeating the purpose of living off the grid altogether.

There are countless other restrictions and ordinances that you need to consider, including those that police livestock, selling vegetables and fruits, and disposing of your sewage waste. Understanding how these can affect your transition will make it easier for you to find a place that's less restrictive of your transition.

The Issue of Income

If you're living off the grid, do you need to continue to make an income? Unless you've got a significant amount of savings in your bank account, then you might have to think of ways to make money while living an otherwise 'backward' life. That cabin won't pay for itself, and neither will all of the other tools and materials you need to fashion your own self-sustaining home.

Off-gridders have found that when they need money the most is actually during the transition itself. As you start to build and design your new off-grid home, you'll need to purchase quite a few items to make sure everything is working smoothly.

The issue lies in the fact that an off-grid lifestyle will typically *not* support traditional employment. Of course, when you work in an office, you should expect to use water and electricity, among other things that aren't permissible in an off-grid lifestyle.

While there are other ways to make money while living off the grid, these can be pretty tricky to understand and execute. Usually, these alternatives involve selling your produce and performing unique services like teaching. Therefore, you should expect it will take quite a bit of getting used to.

Isolation Can Be Overwhelming

Another reason why you might not be able to survive off-grid living alone has less to do with having someone to help you with hard labor and is more about *having someone* period. Often, the most ideal places for off-grid homes are rural areas where commercial establishments are few and far between.

So, before you start planning, you need to accept that it might not be possible to continue to enjoy the things you currently do for fun - like nights out at the bar, family trips to the mall, and brunches with your close friends.

Fortunately, there's an opportunity to make new friends, as off-gridder communities have become particularly accessible and interactive in the past few years. If you're lucky, you might be able to settle in areas where off-grid households are already in operation, and this can significantly help ease your transition and even earn you a friend or two in the process.

Off-Grid in the City - Is It Possible?

Perhaps you feel like living in rural areas isn't for you, perhaps you want to be in a place that feels familiar, or perhaps you simply don't have the funds to buy a plot of land outside the city yet, and all you have to go on is the land that your house is currently sitting on.

In these cases, you may find yourself asking - is it possible to live off the grid in the city? The answer is yes, but there are limits and a few hurdles along the way, so it's important to get creative.

Each county, city, or town has its own regulations, so the rules can change depending on where you live. However, the biggest setback in most urban communities is that disconnecting from the grid is widely prohibited, and local governments will often restrict individuals from going off-grid for safety reasons.

The solution to some urban off-gridders is simply to completely unplug. Without any appliances and electronics plugged into your home, there is essentially no consumption. As for your water, most cities will not allow you to have your water disconnected *if* you have pending unpaid bills.

You can choose to pay off those bills and request to have your water disconnected so that no water supply feeds into your home. You might be wondering - why not just turn off your faucets and valves? Even with all the valves tightly sealed, there is a chance for residual water to leak into your pipes, causing a small amount of consumption each month, so having it turned off from the source can help guarantee zero usage.

If you're interested in developing a self-sustaining home, you need to consider where you will grow your food. Most of the time, city dwellers who've been able to purchase a single family home have enough space in their own backyard to grow enough fruits and vegetables to sustain them all year round.

However, keep in mind that growing produce is one of the main sources of income for people who choose to live off the grid. So, you might want to ensure that you have enough space for fruits and vegetables if you want to be able to sell them and have enough to store for yourself.

Essentially, *an off-grid lifestyle can be attainable*

anywhere in the world. What you need to be aware of is the extent of self-reliance you can have. To some extent, urban households that transition to an off-grid system will still somehow be connected to the grid, albeit with very little dependence.

Adapting to an Off-Grid Mindset

On the surface, your concerns might be more centered on the system of developing an off-grid household, and that's perfectly normal. After all, you will have to learn how to make money, grow food, and manage your utilities without depending on anyone else.

But what a lot of individuals that move into this lifestyle don't anticipate is how *uncomfortable* it can feel - not really when it comes to how you *physically* feel, but more so with how you enjoy your everyday life.

If there's one word that can perfectly encapsulate the process of transitioning to an off-grid lifestyle, it's *downsizing*. There are a lot of things you'll need to sacrifice when you disconnect from the grid - despite being able to find sound alternatives for each one.

For instance, disengaging from traditional electricity means you might not be able to use as many appliances as you typically do. It means you might not find a place or the power to fire up the latest gaming console that you've been dying to play. Also, it means that you might have to settle with just an hour of internet access every day, as opposed to your 24/7 connectivity in your life on the grid.

In essence, living off the grid means *sacrifice*, and living with exactly what you need and nothing more. It means letting go of all the worldly interests you used to have in favor of living a life that is less damaging to the environment. Yes, it's going to be difficult at the beginning. However, having the right mindset before diving into the change can help make the transition a whole lot easier.

So - what is the mindset you should adapt to guarantee a successful move away from the grid? Consider the following key points:

- **It's more than just a fad change.** Sometimes, you might find yourself questioning why you decided to do all of this in the first place - especially when you feel overwhelmed by the new chores and responsibilities that you've taken on. However, what you need to remind yourself of is that *this is more than just a fad change*. What you're doing isn't only for you, but for future generations and the wonderful creatures around us that deserve a healthy ecosystem.

- **You don't need as much as you thought.** People stop living off the grid for one main reason - *it's all work and no play*. There is some truth to this, as living off the grid might make you feel like every day is a chore, without any time to rest or enjoy yourself. But when you put things into perspective, you'll see that what you thought you *needed* to be able to relax wasn't really a necessity in the first place.

Family trips to the mall every weekend, completing stickers from a coffee shop to get your hands on the latest yearly planner that you never actually finish, buying into the latest gadgets and smartphones, eating at new, trendy restaurants that have just opened in town - do you *really* need all of that to feel fulfilled?

The truth is, modern urban life has taught us that we need a plethora of things to be happy and content. But that's far from the truth. In reality, the only things you can call *needs* are those that are essential to your survival, and this includes decent, clean shelter, clothing for different seasons, water, and sufficient amounts of food. Anything that you don't need to survive isn't necessary.

- **Learn to love the outdoors.** Perhaps the greatest defense you can have against the loneliness, isolation, and psychological stress of switching so drastically from the life you used to know is a love for nature.

Once you start living off the grid, the great outdoors will make up a large chunk of your lifestyle - whether that means growing produce in your backyard or trekking away from home to collect water. Learning to appreciate the beauty and simplicity of living a life close to nature can make the transition far easier.

A Few Steps Towards Preparedness

Aside from having the right mindset, it's equally important to have the necessary skills to be able to start out your new lifestyle with as little difficulty as possible. There are quite a few changes you need to adapt to in order to guarantee the seamless completion of chores and responsibilities, and these mainly arise from the fact that you're using alternative sources for the things you use.

Here are a few things you can do to help prepare yourself for the transition:

1. **Adapt a quick strength-enhancing workout plan** - One thing that many don't immediately anticipate is the amount of sheer physical strength needed in order to efficiently accomplish off-grid household management. After all, everything that used to be as simple as flicking a switch now all becomes *manual labor*.

Having said that, the first thing you should consider is observing a fitness routine that maximizes your strength. Remember - managing an off-grid home will essentially take all of your daylight hours and even some that you would prefer to skip in the evening. So, having a strong, healthy body will work to your advantage.

2. **Practice cooking whole foods** - In a self-sustaining household, most of the food you'll eat will come from your own garden. In some cases, when a household is situated in an area where farm animals are prohibited, they might only purchase meat and poultry from their local farmer's market.

Whatever the case, you need to know that whole food will become a large part of your diet. So, you should practice how to cook them, especially in the conditions that you might expect in your off-grid home.

Try out new recipes with fresh produce, avoid buying anything that comes in a can, a plastic bag, or a box, make sure you're using ingredients that are *in season*, and learn how to cook with alternative methods like with firewood and coal.

3. **Read up on growing your own fruits and vegetables** - You'd be surprised just how challenging it can be to actually get some produce growing in your own backyard. Sure, they might

make it seem easy peasy when you read about it online or in books, but plants can be fickle. If you don't care for them to a tee, you might not have any produce when you need it.

Consider prepping your land to grow produce by treating the soil and studying how it's positioned, relative to the sun. There are certain vegetables and fruits that grow better when they get some shade throughout the day, so if your land doesn't have any shaded areas at any given time, then you might have to consider building a partial canopy.

On top of that, it's vital that you learn which fruits and vegetables grow in which seasons. The last thing you'd want is to force a plant to bear produce when it's not their time. Understanding the schedules of these fruits and vegetables will make it easier for you to plan out your growing schedule and optimize your efforts so that you get the most returns out of your land.

4. **Learn how to preserve your own food** - Just because you've managed to harvest more produce than you need, it doesn't necessarily mean that you're in the clear. If your fruits and veggies rot before you can eat them, then you might not have enough food until the next

harvest. If you're moving into the winter, it becomes an even bigger challenge because there might not be a new harvest at all.

The art of preserving food is something you should be very keen to learn about. You can lengthen the shelf life of different foods in many different ways, depending on what works best for that specific kind of produce, whether meat, fish, or poultry.

If during the start of your new lifestyle, you mess up and end up having a bunch of 'preserved' foods that aren't viable to eating, you can run down to the market and buy some food. Remember - there's nothing wrong with making a few mistakes down the line and having to purchase items in order to replace those that you didn't quite manage to get right.

5. **Read how to manage your waste** - From the scraps you collect after you cook a meal, to any wrappers, papers, and bits of recyclables you accumulate over a period of time, to the smelly stuff you push out and into your toilet, waste management is a big part of living off the grid.

Read up on the different processes you might have to perform in order to properly dispose and manage your waste, and consider the different kinds of off-grid toilets you can have in your home. Also, look for recycling centers near your home and find out what items they're willing to take in for you.

Finally, read up on other types of material and whether there are people willing to purchase it from you. Often, metal scraps can be sold for small amounts of money, which is always welcome if you're living off the grid.

6. **Live with the least** - Before you even start your transition, you might want to try living with the *least* to get yourself started in the right direction. This means using as little water and electricity as possible since you won't be living with the same seemingly 'unlimited' supply of utilities anymore.

When you use solar power or convert to battery power when you live off the grid, you'll learn that you can only really use a select number of electronics and appliances at any given time. The reason for this is that these energy sources can only provide you a fraction of what you would be getting if you were still linked in.

It pays to know just how much juice your different devices and household electronics use in order to properly allocate the energy you have. If you plan to have a refrigerator or a deep freezer, you should know that there may not be much else you might be able to fire up, especially if you're only working with a limited supply of energy.

When it comes to water, what you collect is essentially all you have to work with. If you use too much water with each shower, meal prep, laundry, or whatever other chores require water, you might not have enough to see you through the day. The problem here is that collecting water can be particularly difficult, especially if you don't have your own well. In some cases, off-gridders may even have to wait for rain before they can collect water.

Calculate rations and find out how much you consume in a week's time. Add a few extra gallons for safe measure and use this as your benchmark for collecting and using water. If you stay within your calculated numbers and don't face any unexpected changes, you should have enough water every week.

Chapter 2 - I'm Ready to Move!

Now What?

Now that you've understood the basic idea of living off the grid, the next step is figuring out how to execute your plan. There are a variety of variables that will come into play, including the type of dwelling you choose, your location, and how far off the grid you really want to go.

Choosing the Right Property

If you've got a little cheddar to spare or if you plan to sell your current home in order to purchase a new one, there are a few considerations you need to make before you settle on a specific property. The most important ones concern your property's accessibility to alternative utility resources.

Water

A stable, sustainable, and clean water source should be your primary concern. Water will help grow your crops, feed your livestock, keep you clean, and essentially help you accomplish a variety of other chores and tasks around your homestead.

So, how can you tell if your property will be a feasible place to live in terms of water supply? Try answering the following questions:

- Is it in a location that experiences rain on a frequent, regular, and predictable basis?

- Are there streams, ponds, or creeks nearby with fresh water? Do these bodies of natural water ever dry up at any point in the year?

- Can you possibly install a well or a manual water pump?

Generally speaking, you'd want your property to have at least 2 of these factors, and this is because you should always be thinking of contingency plans in case your original plan doesn't work out. If your initial water source is compromised, then you have a secondary choice to draw water from.

You also have to keep in mind that certain areas put limits on the amount of rainwater a resident can collect, and sometimes prohibit it altogether. Other areas deem the collection of rainwater illegal altogether. When it comes to wells, there may also be some restrictions that police the use of groundwater, so make sure to familiarize yourself with the law so that you don't end up violating any ordinances.

Power

Just because you're living off the grid, it doesn't mean that you will no longer need to use electronically-powered devices. There are many reasons to still invest in an alternate electricity source - searching the internet for off-grid solutions, calling up relatives and staying connected with friends, or enjoying an occasional movie with your family.

Here are some methods you can try to generate your own energy:

- **Solar power** - This is the most commonly used alternative because it's the most popular. However, powering an entire home with *just* solar power can be less than economical, although achievable. The infrastructure can be very expensive, as you may need to have a significant number of panels if you want to have enough power for things like a refrigerator.

There have been many recent advances in solar power and the batteries used to store excess power for the evening or cloudy days. I go into greater detail in some of my other books should you want to leverage solar power. I also wrote a book on installing solar power on an RV or trailer should you be looking to live in one of those. This remains a *part* of the solution and not the entire solution on its own, as a combination of power options remains your best bet.

- **Wind power** - If your location allows it, you might want to consider buying a wind turbine. They come in a variety of standard sizes, and the smaller ones are often enough for most residential properties.

The main consideration you need to make is whether there will be a consistent and strong enough breeze to keep your turbines in motion throughout the year. This often depends on your location, as places that are higher up tend to experience more consistent winds.

- **Hydro Power** - Considered one of the most reliable energy sources given that all requirements are met, hydropower can keep your home aptly supplied with energy, with excess to spare. In the right conditions, a water turbine can run 24 hours a day and produce so much power that you have some left to store.

The downside is that the on-site conditions that a water turbine needs might be much more specific than most other power sources. Hydropower needs a constant, reliable source of flowing water in order to generate power, and this might be hard to satisfy because flowing streams are not easy to stumble upon.

Climate and Weather Conditions

Weather and climate change from place to place. Some areas only experience an interchange between rainy and sunny weather, whereas some locations go through all 4 seasons. In most cases, it would be best to look for a location that only switches between rain and sun because it makes growing your produce far more predictable.

The downside, though, is that during the summer, you might not be able to depend on rain as a water source. Sometimes, summer can get so difficult that you might even experience a drought and have to rely on your stored water for long periods of time.

During the rainy season, there might also be a chance of hurricanes. If your property just happens to be in the way of tropical storms and heavy rains, then you might find parts of your home and farm frequently damaged.

In areas where the climate allows all 4 seasons, your biggest concern is winter. During the coldest time of the year, it is impossible to grow any crops and most natural sources of water are frozen. In the same light, you might also struggle to keep yourself warm which means you might want to consider a few unique techniques to stay comfortable during the cold winter months.

There are a variety of online resources you can use to find the weather trends in specific areas. This can help you plan your strategy and let you figure out what you need way before weather conditions get out of hand.

Local Laws and Ordinances

You'd be surprised to know that there are a lot of restrictions and red tape that you might have to go through depending on the county that you choose to live in. In most urban settings, residents are prohibited from disconnecting from the grid and using their own utilities, so it can be difficult to achieve your desired lifestyle.

In most cases, growing your own produce is absolutely acceptable. However, selling it to the public might be prohibited because of the dangers that it poses in terms of health and safety. Also, many cities will call you out for having livestock in your home.

While there's always a way to work around certain ordinances and laws, it's always better to find an area that won't give you such a hard time with permits. If you don't have the resources to move and you're currently living in a place that's heavily guarded by laws and restrictions, brace yourself for long processes and lots of red tape.

Types of Dwellings

Some individuals who transition from the usual lifestyle to an off-grid household do so by first simply 'unplugging' from their home. While this can be a suitable initial solution and a great way to start your transition, you will find yourself wanting to adapt to something more permanent in the long run.

Understanding the kinds of dwellings available and figuring out which one will work best for you will help optimize your budget and guarantee your comfort.

- **RVs or Campers** - Recreational vehicles and campers make suitable dwellings for single off-gridders and couples. These highly manageable mobile homes can be comfortable and easy to maintain, giving you just enough room to house all of the comforts you need - like a bed, a shower, a small dining area, and a kitchen.

  However, living in an RV does come with its own unique set of challenges. For instance, they might not be able to regulate temperatures efficiently, so when it's hot outside, you should expect it to be pretty hot inside too, and of course, the same goes for cold weather.

Another thing you may want to consider is storage space, as RVs and campers - even the biggest ones you can find - often come with limited storage space.

However, as it's likely that you won't be housing an entire family in a small RV, the storage space might just be enough to keep preserved produce for one or two people. If you want to learn more about living in an RV, read up on resources to learn more about the intricacies of this type of lifestyle.

- **Small Cabin Dwellings and Minimalists Houses** – Off-gridders who want more space but don't necessarily want to manage a big house often settle for tiny ones. These permanent residences are easier to hook up to water and sewage systems and offer a more comfortable sense of permanence. Also, smaller houses are easier to power up with solar energy alone, since they are so small.

Many off-gridders try to build their own cabins, but there are restrictions on that too. Some counties won't let people build if the construction changes anything about the property's footprint, even if it's on your own land.

Another benefit of having a tiny home is that it leaves you with far more space to grow your crops and keep your livestock. With more outdoor area, you can allocate more space to different types of fruits and vegetables, and maybe even make room for some trees.

- **Large Solar Powered Homes** - If you've got quite a bit of money to spare, then you might want to consider living in a more spacious place. For some people, living in a large home in the middle of a rural community can be much more comfortable because a wider indoor space allows more room for recreation.

There are a variety of energy sources you can try, but if you have enough money for it, you may want to consider investing in enough solar panels to power your entire home.

Sure, it might seem expensive at the beginning, but there are a few hacks you can put into action to ease the cost. Also, there's a wealth of resources on the topic of solar-powered homes that you can use to ensure seamless operations all year round. My other books are a great starting point.

Deciding How Far Off the Grid You Should Go

Living disconnected can be done in varying degrees. Some people feel more comfortable living closer to the grid, while others prefer living as far away from it as possible. Of course, this depends on how you define comfort and security.

- **Urban** - This type of location puts you right at the center of city life. You might have a few malls and commercial establishments within walking distance and live near offices and other places of work. The urban setting can make it hard to adapt to an off-grid lifestyle simply because it exists *on* the grid.

One of the pros of living in these conditions is that you can always run back to grid-linked utilities. If you somehow end up not saving enough water or power in time for winter, you can just hook back up to the system and use what you need.

The downside to this is that people who live so close to the grid might end up feeling too comfortable, meaning that the environment might not make residents feel too pressured to store and save food and water for down seasons.

- **Semi-Urban** - Semi-urban or suburban communities are mostly residential and feature the typical neighborhood scene you would see in movies. Most residents who live in suburban communities have larger plots of land to work with, giving them more freedom to grow produce.

  However, there are unique restrictions and limitations placed on suburban communities, especially if there's a homeowners' association in operation. On top of that, living so close to other residents in the area might mean that you have to be particularly cautious with your waste management and livestock.

Semi-urban settings also leave you little access to alternate water sources. Even then, you can still have some connection to the grid, so you can easily hook up if you don't store enough of something for the tougher times of the year.

- **Rural** - A farmhouse in the middle of nowhere, with a few neighbors a kilometer or two away - that's what you might call a rural environment. In this setting, you have much more freedom to manage your home because there isn't anyone around to inconvenience or to consider.

Larger plots of land allow more room to grow your crops and care for your animals. Rural areas are also much closer to natural water sources and provide you more space to put up energy sources like wind turbines and solar panels.

In these areas, your biggest problem might be the limitation of resources. As you won't have any connection to the grid, there's no possible way to link back in if you end up storing less than you need. Therefore, it's imperative that you work hard all year round to ensure ample supply in the winter.

- **Full Isolation** - For those who really want to feel closer to nature and as far away from the complications of urban living, a life in full isolation might be ideal. However, keep in mind that completely severing the ties that connect you to other communities can cause certain psychological effects later on in life.

Living in full isolation is often best achieved when you have a support system like a family or a partner to live with. On the upside, living this far away from public utilities means that you'll have the biggest opportunity to reduce your carbon footprint.

On top of that, living in isolation and closer to nature unlocks new experiences that might make you satisfied with the off-grid lifestyle. For instance, living in an urban environment while attempting to unlink from the grid might still expose you to the typical worldly possessions you used to enjoy, making it difficult to fully enjoy your new lifestyle.

On the contrary, living in complete isolation opens your eyes to the perks of living simply, making it easier to appreciate nature and embrace the primary reason for your new lifestyle.

Chapter 3 - Living and Surviving All Year Round

It's definitely going to take quite a bit of time, energy, and effort to fully make the switch to an off-grid lifestyle. So naturally, many people look for ways to help make the switch a little easier. For the most part, the hardest aspect of living off the grid has more to do with food than anything else.

Growing, harvesting, and storing different kinds of produce, wheat, grains, and of course, throwing meat into the mix is something that's completely alien to most of us, thanks to the modern convenience of grocery stores.

Is it wrong to source your food from the supermarket if you're trying to unlink? Of course not. But if you're going to completely fall off the grid, then somewhere down the line, you'll feel that becoming completely self-reliant is an inevitable part of the equation - especially if you're doing all of this to make a change for the global community and the environment.

Hydrate, Hydrate, Hydrate!

There is probably no demographic on earth more highly aware of the value of water than people living off the grid. The process of collecting, storing, and rationing can be backbreaking. But because of its inherent purpose and importance around your homestead, collecting and storing water becomes a major priority on your daily to-do.

Just how important *is* water, you might ask? Consider these uses:

- Personal hygiene

- Growing crops, produce, and caring for other vegetation

- For livestock and other animals

- Household cleaning

- Cooking and meal prep

- Laundry

- For quenching your thirst - which you'll feel more often now that you're exerting lots of physical effort to keep your home well managed.

A lot of these tasks might seem easy because you're already familiar with them, but if you factor in the reality that water *is not unlimited* when you're living off the grid, then you'll learn why it becomes a challenge. What you collect is essentially all you have to work with, so if you don't have enough of it, you might have to scratch a few items off of your list.

To complicate matters further, it's worth mentioning that water isn't as easily collected as you think. You can always just run down to the nearby stream or pond, you say. But what if you're on a property that isn't near one? Then maybe you can install a well. But do you have the money it takes to have one dug up, which costs roughly $10,000 - $15,000 USD? Well, if not, maybe you'll just have to wait for the next downpour. But what if it's the summer, and it isn't expected to rain for two months?

The truth is, most off-gridders find themselves using a large fraction of their day trying to replenish water stores and building their stash for the dry seasons. So, optimizing your strategy and making sure that you're doing everything right will help guarantee clean, usable, stored water that's enough to see you through the summer or winter.

Practical Water Collection for Drinking

Drinking water is collected and processed differently than utility water. That's because drinking water needs to be particularly purified and filtered since there might be some microbes and bacteria in it that could cause disease and illness. Also, storage is different since you'd want to keep it clean even after having it stowed away for several months.

For the most part, every source of natural freshwater you'll find, whether from a well, a moving stream, or even the rain requires some cleaning and filtration in order to be drinkable. So, you might need a few tools or pieces of equipment to help you process water in bulk to store it for drinking.

Store-Bought Filtration System

If you've got an extra buck or two to spare, you might want to invest in a store-bought water filtration system. These things can filter large sums of water daily, and they require very little maintenance and manual operation. Of course, they do use up quite a bit of electricity, which means you'd have to factor that into your power consumption. But otherwise, they are exceptionally effective, shaving off the steps needed for you to get access to safe drinking water.

Natural Filtration with Fruits

Do you usually toss your fruit peelings in the trash? Why not toss it in your water instead? Science has discovered that the peel on most fruits can act as powerful filtration agents, cleaning out a wide range of contaminants and heavy metals. There are a variety of fruit peelings you can use, including banana peels (which can be used to filter water up to 11 times), apple and tomato peels, and coconut fiber and rice husks.

The downside? Of course, by filtering your water with fruit, you will somehow infuse some of its flavor. So, your water might not have the same, satisfying, 'tasteless' quality that you are used to. Nonetheless, it will be safe to drink, which is good enough for most people.

Solar Disinfection

While it's rarely considered a long-term solution to filtered water, solar disinfection can work to give you clean, drinkable water. However, you have to remember that this method of filtration only works if you have relatively clear water, because it can't remove sediments.

The process works by placing clear water in clear plastic bottles and exposing it to direct sunlight for at least 24 hours. This is best accomplished by placing the bottles on your roof. Once the process is done, the water can be drinkable thanks to the disinfecting properties of UV rays.

In the same way, off-gridders can also invest in UV light treatment. The process uses the same principle as sunlight disinfection and poses a much more long-term solution to keep your water clean. Of course, it does cost quite a bit to have the machine installed at home, but it will easily reduce the time and effort you'd typically use to clean your water.

Ceramic Water Filter

If you want a solution that's easy on the pocket but can still process large amounts of water at a time, you might want to consider a ceramic water filter. These contraptions can be easily made at home, and they're exceptionally effective at removing contaminants from fresh water.

The DIY design involves placing a ceramic pot inside a water container, leaving enough space between them. As the ceramic pot filters the water, it drips through the ceramic material's small pores and trickles down into the container underneath. Once all the water is filtered, it is collected into the container, clean and ready to be drunk.

You can purchase store-bought ceramic filters, but they really aren't any different in terms of efficacy, and doing it yourself with a ceramic pot and a container can be much cheaper. If you need to filter more water at a time, consider getting larger pots and containers, or multiplying the number of filtration units you make.

Storing Drinking Water

It's important to make sure that you keep your drinking water in safe containers with no risk of re-contamination. This is especially important if you plan to store them for long periods of time, such as throughout a drought, when water might not be accessible and you'll need to rely on what you've been able to store.

<u>Short-term Drinking Water Storage</u>

Your short-term water supply is the drinking water you expect to consume within 1-3 days. You might keep it in your kitchen or fridge, and it's likely what you will use to quench your thirst.

Using polyethylene terephthalate (PET) plastic bottles that have been previously used to contain other beverages like sodas can be a viable solution. To sanitize the bottles, create a bleach and clean water solution with a ratio of 1 teaspoon of household liquid bleach to each gallon of water. Fill the bottle up to the cap, and seal tightly.

After 2 minutes, pour the solution out of the bottle, and with potable drinking water, rinse out the inside of each bottle. Then, fill each one with your potable drinking water.

Long-term Drinking Water Storage

High-density polyethylene plastic bottles - similar to those used for milk and juice - are hard-wearing, highly resistant to extreme daytime temperatures, and chemically resistant. They're structurally sound and hold very well against long-term storage, keeping water potable and clean even after months of being stagnant.

HDP bottles can be purchased in 5-gallon sizes, making them ideal for storing large amounts of drinking water. Some feature a faucet attachment that makes it easier to take water from each bottle, but these do make them prone to re-contamination. Consider using the plain bottles to store water for the long-term.

Practical Water Collection for Hygiene

Soon, you will realize that a number of the tasks you will do day in and day out require the use of water. From cleaning your house, to tending to your garden, to making sure all your laundry is in proper order, water is something that needs to be available in abundance at all times if you want to keep your homestead running properly.

Fortunately, water collected from streams, wells, and other natural sources of freshwater should be clean enough to be used for a variety of household chores. If there's a clean source of freshwater near your home, then you might not have to store any to get *today's* responsibilities done.

For the most part, people who store utility water do so to prepare for a few possible hitches in the homestead plan:

- Calamities or accidents affecting the viability of the water source

- Gaps in water availability such as during the dry season or if the water freezes during winter

- In case of fires and other emergencies that might require the use of water

Having said that, it's important to make sure you have at least some water in storage for those unforeseen instances in your homestead management experience. Fortunately, there are quite a few ways you might be able to build your stash.

Rainwater Collection System

In some counties, it's illegal to collect rainwater. The reason for this is that it is seen as a health and safety hazard, especially because rainwater could become a breeding ground for disease-carrying mosquitoes. Ensure to check with your local laws to find out whether rainwater collection is a viable solution for your homestead.

If it is, then it's time that you invest in a rainwater collection system. These contraptions can be as large as your typical water barrel or as gigantic as an underground water cistern - it all depends on what you need. Having said that, there are three different kinds of rainwater collection systems:

- **Rainwater barrel** - These barrels can collect anywhere from 50 to 100 gallons, and are simply water storage barrels that are positioned at the end of rain gutters. Each gutter should have one barrel underneath it in order to make the most of the rainfall. The challenge here is relocating or replacing the barrels once they're full.

- **Dry Water System** - A dry water system uses a design that's similar to the rainwater barrel, with the exception that the collection cistern can't be moved from its place, even when it's full. It's called a dry system because the pipe completely dries up after every downpour. The benefit is that cisterns can be much larger than typical rainwater barrels.

- **Wet Collection System** - The wet collection system is probably the largest of all rainwater storage systems. This design uses a large, single cistern where all gutters connect via an intricate network of pipes. The benefit is that you don't have to manually bring all the collected water together since they're all funneled into a single containment. On the other hand, the downside is that the pipes might require some maintenance to prevent contamination.

Groundwater Collection System

If you're lucky enough to have groundwater access on your property, a well or a pump are great investments to have on your homestead. While it can be expensive to have the land dug up in the first place, groundwater is highly reliable and constant, providing you with a clean source of sustainable water for many years to come.

For the most part, collecting water from under the ground requires a well or a pump. Some homesteads use electric water pumps to ease the process of collection, but because they do require quite some power, you might want to consider using a manual pump instead.

Fuel Your Body

Next, let's talk about fruits and vegetables. Considered the staple food for off-grid homesteaders, growing your own produce can mean that you'll have access to an ample food supply all year round.

Of course, we all dream of having a bountiful farm full of fresh fruit and vegetables, but it's not easy to turn that dream into reality. In fact, growing produce can be a lot harder than most experienced off-grid homesteaders make it seem.

How to Grow Your Own Produce

Every vegetable requires different conditions to grow. Partial light, partial shade, weather conditions, specific temperatures, calculated amounts of water - there are a lot of different factors you'll need to consider for each plant you want to grow.

Having said that, you need to ensure that you and your land are both prepared to care for the variety of produce you intend to grow. So what do you need?

Essentials for Growing Vegetables

- **Seeds or Cuttings** - Of course, you're going to need something to start your plants from. Seeds can easily be purchased from grocery stores or taken directly from the fruits and vegetables you eat at home. In some cases, it might be easier to grow a plant from a cutting instead of a seed, especially if you have limited experience growing your own plants. If you know anyone or anywhere you can get plant cuttings from, try to source those first before you try your hand at seeds.

- **Garden tools** - A pair of garden shears, wheelbarrow, hoe, spade, dibbler, rake, shovel, and a garden hose are all important essentials that you should have in your arsenal. As your garden grows and you discover new tricks, you might want to add a few other tools to the mix.

- **Water supply** - Your garden should have its own designated water allocation. So, from all the water you collect from your source, you should make sure to factor in your garden's water needs, especially if you don't expect a lot of rain. The amount of water depends on the size of your garden as well as the kind of plants you plan to grow.

- **Shade** - While it's always nice to have some warm sun shining down on your garden, there are specific amounts of sunlight that a plant should get over a 24 hour period. Some plants grow better in partial sun, and others in partial shade. To ensure you have the proper conditions to accommodate a variety of plants, consider having a retractable canopy or a removable umbrella installed over a strategic location in your garden.

Best Types of Veggies to Grow

While there isn't really a 'best' kind of veggie, there are some that are easy to grow and offer just the right nutritional values to meet your dietary needs. These produce choices are ideal inclusions for your garden because they provide fast returns, a lot of variety, and require the least possible maintenance, making them easy choices for off-grid homesteaders.

- **Radishes** - These root crops can grow in as little as 21 days, and offer unique textures and flavors that are ideal for a variety of recipes. They're exceptionally nutritious and particularly easy to grow, which is why they're often one of the most popular choices for off-grid homesteads.

- When it comes to conditions, radishes aren't picky, and they'll grow in almost any season minus the winter. However, they do grow best in temperatures between 50°F and 65°F. Three to four days after planting, you should see radish sprouts peeking up from the soil. These can be planted weekly or every two weeks to have a steady supply at any given time.

- **Lettuce** - This salad staple can be ready in as little as 30 days. The great thing is that you don't have to uproot the entire plant to get what you need - just snip away the leaves you need and leave the rest of the plant to grow further throughout the season. If you want a constant supply of lettuce, try planting new cuttings every 14 days.

- **Spinach** - If you live in a particularly cold area, you might want to grow spinach. This resilient vegetable can survive temperatures as cold as 15°F, grows relatively quickly, and can be harvested just 30 days after being planted. To guarantee a stable supply, re-sow the seeds every two weeks.

- **Turnips** - Mature turnips take about 2 months to harvest, but pulling them out of the ground 30 days after being planted will give you small, sweet, and mild veggies that are perfect for soups and salads. On top of that, you can also cut the leafy sprouts off to add to sautéed vegetables and leave the rest of the root crop to grow to full size.

- **Carrots** – It can take up to 50 days for a carrot to reach mature size, but it's also possible to harvest them sooner if you want baby carrots. Sweet and crunchy carrots can be spaced closely together if you want to harvest them while small, leaving you more room to grow a variety of other crops.

- **Tomatoes** - Tomatoes are juicy, versatile, and flavorful, making them wonderful additions to your favorite soups, sautés, and other recipes. They grow best in hot climates and love having lots of sun, so there's no need to consider shade when trying to propagate them. They grow from the summer to the beginning of winter, so ensure to grow them in large amounts and preserve them properly to see you through the colder months. It can take between 60 to 80 days to harvest ripe tomatoes.

- **Onions** - Adding a ton of flavor to any recipe

or meal, onions are a staple in most households - whether off the grid or linked in. To grow them, you can opt to plant seeds or start from bulblets which are much easier to work with. Depending on the variety of onion you choose, it can take between 20 and 175 days before you can harvest a mature onion. In the meantime, you can snip the leeks and add them to soups and other recipes.

- **Garlic** - Aside from being a tasty addition to a variety of meals, garlic is also commonly used in a variety of home remedies. While they might take quite some time to reach maturity - up to 9 months - garlic lasts very long even without a lot of preservation effort.

How to Store Harvested Veggies

It's one thing to grow and harvest your veggies, and another thing to keep them well stored. Remember, your objective is to make sure that they last as long as possible, and through the seasons when you might not be able to grow them. This will help guarantee that your household always has a variety of produce choices to enjoy even when it's not their time of the year.

- As a general rule, **green leafy vegetables do not store well**. The best way to keep them fresh for longer would be to wrap them in paper towels, then place them in a plastic bag. This should then be stored in a cool place like a fridge. Cut off leaves as you need them and return the rest of the vegetable in the fridge to cool. If you don't have a fridge, make sure the vegetables are dry, wrap them in a paper towel, and store them in a dry, sealed container.

- Vegetables like **zucchini and cucumbers** can last as long as 3 weeks if you keep them in a fridge. If you keep them any longer than that, they will start to get rubbery and mushy. Because they bruise easily, you can pickle them instead with brine made from vinegar and salt.

- In the right conditions, onions and garlic **can last for up to 6 months** (i.e. cooler with less humidity.) Clean out any dirt that may be on the skins and keep them in a mesh bag. Hang this in your kitchen and take onions or garlic as needed.

-

- **Avoid storing any sort of vegetables** along with your fruits. Veggies tend to hasten the ripening of fruits, and thus shorten their shelf life. The same goes for storing potatoes with onions which may cause the former to sprout.

- Most **root crops are best stored in a dry, dark place**. Place clean root crops that are free of dirt in clean paper bags and store them in a dark space with no humidity.

- If you notice that any of your vegetables are starting to ripen off schedule, you can always pickle them or turn them into sauces, jams, or spreads. There are a variety of recipes that illustrate many different ways you can turn your over-ripened vegetables into something completely new - so don't be afraid to get creative.

Growing Your Own Fruits and Nuts

Sweet, succulent, and tremendously tricky to stop munching on, fruits and nuts are a grand indulgence for people living off the grid. These delicious additions to your pantry help guarantee that there is always something to satisfy your sweet tooth and something to replace those store-bought chips for movie nights.

Essentials for Growing Fruits and Nuts

- **Pest control** - Compared to vegetables, fruits are typically more prone to pests, with lots of different kinds of insect larvae among others burrowing into fruit before you can even manage to harvest them. Learning more about the different types of pest control strategies - from decoys to homemade sprays - can make it easier to avoid the onslaught of pests.

- **Garden plan** - It might feel compelling to stuff as many plants and trees into your garden as possible, but an overcrowded plot might not bear any fruit at all. Make sure you plan out the spacing between each tree, bush, and plant to make sure that they all get the sun and space they need to flourish and grow.

Keep in mind that fruit and nut bearing trees and bushes require far less maintenance than vegetables, but because they typically grow in this form, they might take up a lot of space in your garden.

On the upside, having a tree in your lot will help reinforce the stability of your land and keep it firm throughout a storm. On top of that, having a tree or a bush means you won't have to re-sow anything to have the fruits or nuts growing again.

Best Kinds of Fruits and Nuts to Grow

- **Raspberries, Blueberries, and Strawberries** - Considered some of the easiest sweet treats to grow in your garden, these three types of fruit can be grown in containers. Of course, they'll only be ready to harvest in the summer, but they do make excellent snacks and are even suitable base ingredients for a variety of desserts.

- **Apples** - An apple tree is no simple asset, and is definitely something you might want to have in your garden. However, you should ensure that you choose the right kind of apple tree based on your space and preferences. If you have enough land to offer, consider having at least two different kinds of apples so they can pollinate each other. Alternatively, individuals with smaller land areas can settle for a dwarf family apple tree which can grow three different kinds of apple at the same time.

- **Grapes** - The reason why grapes make such a smart addition to your garden is two-fold - firstly because they're particularly versatile as they can be used in salads, eaten as a standalone snack, juiced, or turned into jams and jellies or even wine. The second reason is that they grow on vines, so they won't take up a lot of space in your garden. While growing grapes is not actually that hard, you will have to consider the fact that they attract quite a lot of birds. So, there will be some stiff competition once harvest time comes rolling around the corner.

- **Watermelons** - If you don't have a lot of space to spare in your garden, you can grow watermelons in containers. These grow best in lots of heat and sunshine, so they make ideal summer fruits. The upside is that once they're harvested and the summer season is done, you can allot the containers or the space they were growing in to other fruits for the colder weather.

- **Lemons** - A lemon tree can be grown in a pot as a dwarf tree, or as a full-sized tree in your lot. They are great to have around as they're used for several home remedies. On top of that, lemons are also known for their cleaning and disinfecting properties, making them an ideal household cleaning ingredient for eco-friendly cleaning formulations.

- **Pistachios** - A pistachio tree measures around 5 meters wide and 5 meters tall, making it a smart addition to smaller spaces. Male and female flowers grow on separate trees, so you might need at least 2 to be able to pollinate and produce nuts. They take well to extremely hot summers and very cold winters, and survive well even on poor soil. You can expect a well-maintained tree to produce nuts in 4 to 5 years.

- **Macadamias** - Velvety and smooth, macadamias are a well-known and loved snack around the world. These delicious nuts grow on trees that are up to 25 feet tall in the wild but will most likely grow to be just around 8 to 10 feet tall in a garden. They take a while to reach maturity from seed, so it's best to purchase a graft instead.

- **Almonds** - These trees can be as compact as just 3 meters in height, so they're great for space saving homes. On top of that, almonds are also particularly versatile, with many uses in both sweet and savory recipes. There should be at least 2 almond trees in your property if you want to produce nuts unless you're lucky enough to find self-fertile varieties.

- **Peanuts** - The 'peanut' name is actually a misnomer since they're actually legumes and not nuts. Nonetheless, they're enjoyed like nuts which is why they've made the list. Peanuts grow best in warm climate under the soil, which makes them a great solution for homesteads with limited space. They can be harvested within 17 weeks of planting and can be prepared and eaten in a number of different ways.

How to Store Harvested Fruits and Nuts

- Generally, **nuts store better than any other food you might grow**. Unshelled nuts can be kept in a fridge for up to 6 months, and in a freezer for up to 12 months. When they're shelled, nuts can be kept in storage for up to 3 months. Dried nuts have an even longer shelf life, lasting over a year in the right conditions.

Make sure to keep all of your nuts in air-tight containers to maintain their freshness and moisture level.

- Fruits are best stored and preserved by **canning, drying, or freezing.** Canning fruits can be done by placing them in a sterilized glass jar - such as a mason jar - and then adding enough boiling water to fill the jar up to an inch below the rim. Use a spoon or spatula to remove air bubbles from the walls of the jar, and then tightly seal. Drying fruits can extend their lifespan significantly. If you have an area that receives constant, bright sunlight throughout the day, you can place your fruits there to dehydrate. You can also use an oven to achieve the same effect. Finally, freezing fruits can suspend them in their current state, so be sure to avoid choosing fruits that have ripened a little too much. Frozen fruit can be kept in storage for 6 to 12 months, depending on how cold it is.

- If all else fails, remember that you can always turn fruits into jams and jellies. Alternatively, some fruits can be fermented and turned into wine or other kinds of drinks, which is the final stage of their lifetime, and they get better as the years roll on.

Growing Your Own Wheat and Grains

As the original source of carbohydrates, wheat and grains will help keep you feeling full and energized. Making these a large portion of your daily diet will ensure that you don't end up feeling hungry, and will guarantee that each meal is satisfying and fulfilling.

Essentials for Growing Wheat and Grains

- **Blanket or Tarp** - Most grains need to be dried to separate the grain from the husk. A large tarp or blanket will provide ample space for you to be able to do this after harvesting your grains.

- **Scythe** - Needed to cut the wheat or grain at the stalk, the scythe will ease the process of harvesting and prevent you from having to go in with your bare hands.

- **Mill** - There are a variety of mill designs available, and some are even small enough to sit on your kitchen counter. These

contraptions help separate the grain husk
from the grain itself.

- **Bucket** - Buckets are necessary to collect your
  grain. Without the proper transport container,
  you might find it impossible to take your
  harvest from one space to another without
  losing a significant amount along the way.

- **Rake** - Used to spread grain across a tarp or to
  collect them in one pile for easier transport
  and processing.

Best Kinds of Wheat to Grow

- **Common wheat** - Used to make the flour we
  use for bread, common wheat is easy to grow
  and harvest. It can also be used for pasta,
  although **durum wheat** is often considered
  more appropriate, offering better outcomes
  for different kinds of raised bread and pasta
  noodles. There are some types of wheat that
  can grow in the winter, which you can
  interchange with summer varieties to make
  sure you have something to harvest as soon as
  the

- cold season is done.

- **Corn** - Corn is versatile and can be used to make cornmeal or flour. It requires a long period of time to grow and it usually does best in hot climates. On top of that, corn needs to be spaced quite far from other vegetables, since they might cross-pollinate. They're typically ideal for homesteads with more space and in areas with long, dry summers.

- **Oats** - Most types of oats grow best in cooler weather, and there are some that are hull-less, making them easier to process after harvest. Oats can be used for baking and for breakfast recipes, offering a large amount of carbohydrates to keep you full and satiated for extended periods of time.

- **Rye** - If you commonly experience difficult, cold, and wet weather in your area, you might be able to grow rye. This grain develops well in poor soil and is an ideal choice for beginners who have no experience growing their own grains.

- **Rice** - Rice makes a great addition to an off-grid homestead because it's packed with carbohydrates and can be enjoyed along with savory meals. However, they're more ideal for properties with *lots* of space, since they require quite a bit of land to grow and thrive. They also require at least 40 days of consistently hot weather, above 70°F.

Storing Harvested Grains

Fortunately, storing your grains might not be as complicated as other types of foods. For the most part, after they've been milled, different types of grain can be kept in airtight containers and clean tubs with reliable seals to keep them fresh and viable. If anything, your biggest challenge would be to keep pests away, since rodents particularly enjoy eating grains.

Keeping and Hunting Animals

If you've successfully transitioned to your off-grid lifestyle and feel confident in your capability to grow fruits and vegetables, it's time to try raising livestock. Animals provide protein which is essential for muscle strength and may be able to supply you with other food sources like eggs and milk.

Essentials for Keeping and Hunting Animals

- **Proper cages and shelter** - You can't just have your livestock moving around your property into any area they please, especially if you're trying to care for a fruit and vegetable garden. Therefore, it is essential to have proper cages and shelter to contain your animals if you want to separate them from your produce.

- **Feed and water** - Different animals eat different kinds of feed and providing them the kind that they need will help ensure rich, healthy meat and animal by-products. In the same light, you also need to factor in the water you will need to keep their homes clean and to keep the animals well hydrated throughout the year.

- **Rakes and shovels** - Animals will poop and make a mess, so ensure to have the right stuff to keep their area clean. A wheelbarrow might also be necessary to move their essentials around.

- **Slaughter shed and tools** - Slaughtering an animal can get messy, so you need to make sure that you have a separate place to do the deed. If you have bigger animals like cows and goats, you need to consider the kind of method you want to implement since smaller tools might not work as easily.

- **Supplements and vitamins** - Animals that you use as workers around your property, like horses should be kept in peak condition in order for them to work as best as they can. Those that are used for their by-products or their meat need to be kept healthy in order to produce high-quality food. Animal supplements and vitamins will give you the necessary micronutrients to ensure proper health.

Best Kinds of Animals to Keep and Hunt

- **Chickens** - Fairly easy to acquire and care for, chickens propagate and grow fast. On top of that, they also lay eggs which can be used for a wide variety of recipes. In some cases, off-grid homesteaders choose not to kill their chickens and instead keep them just for their eggs.

- **Goats** - Goats are sometimes used for their meat, but it does take quite some experience to cook them. They also produce milk, which can be used for consumption or things like creating soap. Goats need quite a bit of care, including vaccinations and deworming if you want to ensure they're kept in good shape.

- **Sheep** - Rarely kept for their meat, sheep bring one smart essential to the table – wool, which can be used to create a number of different essentials like clothing and household necessities. Also, wool can be sold for extra income. Sheep require quite a bit of care and maintenance, and should be sheared on a regular schedule which can be tricky if you've never raised them before.

- **Rabbits** - Working as natural grass cutters, rabbits can eat away at anything and keep your land well kept and maintained. Their pelt can be used to make clothing and other crafts, and their meat is delicious. Of course, the downside is that rabbits can be pretty cute which makes it hard to slaughter them.

- **Pigs** - If you want a great, big source of meat, consider growing pigs on your land. They do require quite a bit more care and investment from homesteaders, but they do pay off. Female pigs will have at least 3 litters a year with as many as 10 piglets per litter. The excess can be sold for a handsome amount, and slaughtering a single pig can produce enough meat to last several months.

- **Fish** - You can keep fish on your property if you've got the infrastructure for it, or you can be smart and simply catch them on your own. Freshwater fish are easy to catch and may be found in large amounts in nearby streams, ponds, or lakes.

- **Wild animals** - Homesteaders have the option to hunt animals in the wild. Of course, hunting poses a unique sort of excitement, especially for those who enjoy the thrill of stalking and capturing their prey. The downside is that it is never guaranteed that you'll come back from a hunt successful.

Most homesteaders actually prefer keeping their own animals at home as this makes them much easier to access. Nonetheless, you can engage in hunting as long as you follow the laws and ordinances that govern your locality. Some hunters also like going for smaller critters like wild hares, ducks, and other types of birds since they're easier game and much less time consuming to hunt. They can be caught with traps or hunted traditionally with a rifle.

Storing and Preserving Animal Meat and Animal Products

- Fortunately, you don't need to store eggs for the winter if the conditions for your hens are right. Ensuring that they get enough warmth during the colder seasons will help them produce eggs even when the temperature dips. Having said that, laid and collected eggs can be kept in storage for up to 5 weeks.

- Milk from your livestock can be viable for only up to 2 weeks after it's collected, and ensuring the sanitation of your milk after collection can help extend its shelf life. Alternatively, you can process the milk and turn it into butter or cheese in order to prolong its use.

- Animal meat can be stored in freezers to extend its freshness for up to a year. Beef jerky - when dried properly - can last up to 2 years in storage.

- Salting is another method for preserving meat. Layering slabs of meat with curing salt and placing them in air-tight jars can keep the meat fresh for up to 4 months. This can be long enough to see you through the winter or until you have other animals that are ready for slaughter.

Outlasting the Winter

The time of year when you might experience the greatest challenge is during winter. In the dead cold of the snowy season, you'll learn that crops will cease to grow, the budding harvest will rot and retreat, animals might experience illness and even death, and water will be hard to source. However, aside from all of these challenges, the hurdle of surviving the cold without the convenience of electricity to heat your home might introduce a new kind of difficulty into your humble homestead.

Ensuring Enough Power

At the start of the year, it should have been your priority to store excess energy in batteries - whether taken from solar panels, wind turbines, or hydropower. After all, preparation is the name of the game and mindset of practically all off- gridders.

On top of that, if you don't expect to get a lot of power during the day, you might want to switch to alternate sources of energy. For instance, you might have to cook on firewood stoves instead of your traditional electric hotplate. This won't only reduce the amount of energy you use, but will also keep your home nice and toasty.

During the day, be sure to collect whatever power you can. Turn off all electronically powered gadgets and devices, and keep usage to a bare minimum. Solar panels and wind turbines should continue to generate power even in the winter, as long as the conditions are met. Also, storing power in batteries is important to see you through the days when collecting power might not be viable.

Hydropower infrastructure might completely halt, especially if water is stagnant and frozen, so ensure that you have alternate energy sources to draw power from if you rely mainly on hydropower.

Keeping the House Warm

Without your traditional HVAC system running throughout your house, you might find that the cold can easily seep through your walls. So, it's important that you have firewood ready before winter.

If there aren't any logs around your home to cut down, you can probably find cheap lumber elsewhere. Some people sell lumber for as cheap as $20 per ton since these are usually scraps from wood that's already been turned into slabs. Cut them up into smaller chunks that you can chuck into the fire in the cold winter season.

To keep the cold breeze out, you might also want to consider placing thick blankets over your windows. Wool from your livestock or blankets purchased from stores can be good enough to help maintain the temperature in your home. Also, readily boiled water kept in a thermos can be used for a quick cup of coffee or to heat up a bath.

Staying Warm With the Right Clothes

In the winter, you won't experience as much sweating, so doing the laundry might not be such a major concern, except of course when it comes to your underwear. What's more, drying up your laundry in the cold of winter could take exceptionally long due to the temperature.

Consider stocking up on blankets, socks, jackets, mittens, and other cold clothing essentials before the winter strikes. If you have livestock that provides pelt, you can harvest it during the warmer seasons and fashion them into winter wear to be prepared for the cold months of.

Also, remember that animals need warmth. When exposed to excessively cold temperatures, most livestock is known to die or become gravely ill. Prepare their shelters for the onslaught of winter and ensure that they have the right provisions to keep them warm too, such as blankets, beddings, and insulated homes.

Rationing Your Food Supply

Considered one of the trickiest parts of surviving the winter, rationing and making sure you have enough food to see you through the cold months can be a challenge. For the most part, you should have been able to generate enough food for your daily needs *as well* as for the winter during the warmer seasons, preserving and storing excess in preparation for the time when growing and harvesting might be more of a challenge.

Properly preserved and stored food - ranging from vegetables to meats - should last at least 3 months, which can be long enough to see you through the coldest days of the winter season. However, during this time, you might also want to consider growing fruits, vegetables, and other crops that are known to grow even in the cold. Furthermore, if you have the ability to create a greenhouse, you can grow smaller amount of fruits and veggies year-round!

Aside from that, it's also important to have enough food stored for your livestock and pets. Consider measuring the amount of food they eat in a week by weight and then calculating how much it would take to feed them for an entire winter. You should have this on hand before the onset of the cold season to ensure your animals survive.

To help ensure you have enough food throughout the entire season, prepare a meal plan using the different ingredients you have at home. Write down menus for each day of the week and ration food so that you're satisfied but still left with enough to keep you going for the rest of the season.

If all else fails and you sense that there might be a shortage before the end of the season, then it's okay to run down to the grocery store to stock up on more food. If you live close to the outskirts, then you should make sure to think ahead and develop a contingency plan way before your food supply runs out.

Remember - it's all about thinking ahead. Imagine every possible worst case scenario and develop a plan to bypass the possible outcomes.

Conclusion

Our lifestyle has made it difficult to imagine the world any other way than how we've come to know it. The convenience of being able to access *everything* with nothing more than the flick of a switch or the turn of a faucet can make it difficult to truly understand just how important and valuable these things actually are.

Is it inherently bad to live life with these conveniences? As a matter of fact, it isn't. There are millions of people who need these utilities the way the grid provides them. The elderly, the sick, the disabled - these people are at a disadvantage and thus they benefit significantly from the ease of access that the modern day system provides.

As for the rest of us, there is a deeper, more critical calling waiting to be answered. Are we willing to keep mooching off of these utilities, enjoying their convenience, and sweeping our accountability under the rug? Do we feel like the ease of our everyday lives outweighs the damage we cause to mother Earth because of the way we've learned to overlook the value of the utilities we enjoy?

According to the WWF, our generation is the *last* generation that has the opportunity to save Mother Nature. So the time to act is *now*.

The truth is, it won't be easy, and you might feel tired and choked with responsibilities more often than not. You might want to return to the way things used to be and give up, thinking you're not making much of a difference anyway. But remember - you matter. The environment matters. And every drop of water you collect, every vegetable you grow, every last bit of waste you process on your own, is all a step closer to making the world a better place for the generations after you.

Surrender your fear and apprehension, trust your instincts, and choose a life that's compassionate, accountable, and free. *This is what it means to be living off the grid.*

Don't forget,

if you like my book,

or even if you don't,

I want to hear about it!

I encouraged you to leave

A review on Amazon.

Help others decide to buy!

EXTRA BONUS!

Thanks for purchasing *Off Grid Living: A Beginners Guide to Surviving and Thriving In An Off Grid Lifestyle.* As a bonus and thanks, we want to provide you with additional information and content on an on-going basis.

Subscribe <u>now</u> and to learn **10 Ways to Downsize Your Current Life – and SAVE MONEY!**

Choose the NEW YOU
www.bit.ly/offgridoffer

Simply type the above link into any web browser on any device.

MY OTHER BOOKS!

Like this one? Check out some of my others!

DIY RV Solar Power: How To Install Your Own Solar Power System For Your RV, Camper, or Boat

Solar Power: How to Harness the Sun to Power Your Life – and Go Off-Grid While Doing It

Solar Power: Making the Smart Switch to Solar Power – and Staying Within Budget

Off Grid Solar Power Living: An EnHanced Guide To Move Your House, RV, Camper, or Boat to Solar Power (TWO BOOKS IN ONE)

How To Install Solar Power: A Comprehensive Guide to Cost Effective Installations of Your Solar Power Needs (TWO BOOKS IN ONE)

Solar Power For Everyone: Unlocking The Keys To Solar Power – From The Beginninger, The DIYer, Or The Advanced Person (THREE BOOKS IN ONE)

Off Grid Solar Power Living MOBILE EDITION: Using Your RV or Camper – And The Sun – To Go Completely Minimalist and Live Off The Grid Year Round